Herbs

Jane Eastoe

Herbs

*Inspiration and practical advice
for gardeners*

 THE NATIONAL TRUST

First published in the United Kingdom in 2009 by
National Trust Books
10 Southcombe Street
London W14 0RA
An imprint of Anova Books Company Ltd

ISBN 9781905400836

A CIP catalogue for this book is available from the British Library.

10 9 8 7 6 5 4 3 2 1

Reproduction by Mission Productions Ltd, Hong Kong
Printed and bound by WS Bookwell Oy, Finland

This book can be ordered direct from the publisher at the website
www.anovabooks.com, or try your local bookshop. Also available at
National Trust shops and www.nationaltrustbooks.co.uk.

CONTENTS

INTRODUCTION

The technical definition of a herb is any aromatic plant that can be used for food and medicine, scent or flavour. It encompasses many thousands of plants, from familiar culinary herbs such as parsley, sage, rosemary and thyme to those with lower gastronomic profiles such as orach, sorrel and lovage. It includes plants many may consider common garden weeds. These aromatic leaves, flowers, roots and seeds have been used for many thousands of years: herbs provided nutrition, flavouring, medicine, dyes and cosmetics from the moment man started gathering as well as hunting.

Herbs are powerful plants: they are packed with nutrients, vitamins and minerals. Some form the basis of important drugs: yew, foxglove and poppy are the sources of the cancer treatment taxol, the heart drug digitalis and the painkiller morphine respectively. However, the focus of this book is on culinary herbs: beautiful, fragrant plants that have the power to transform the simplest dish. An omelette takes only a moment to make, but add a *fines herbes* mix (parsley, chervil, chives and the merest hint of tarragon) and you will have a meal fit for a prince – or even the most demanding restaurant critic.

Our ancestors used herbs on a daily basis, but, with the industrialisation of food processing, the British fell out of the habit. My parents, born at the start of the 20th century, were typical of their generation. Food was plain and simple and, while they grew some fruit and vegetables, herbs were not part of the package, the only exception being an unruly patch of mint, which was regularly raided for mint sauce. But there was no parsley, bay, sage or thyme and the rosemary was purely decorative. They would not have dreamt of using garlic.

The British appear to be the only nation whose culinary history was affected by such a herbal blip. Herbs form a central part of the native diet in Mediterranean and Scandinavian countries, as well as in Africa, Asia, China and the Americas. Betty MacDonald waxes lyrical about the power of herbs in her autobiographical story *The Egg and I*, written in America back in the mid-1940s:

> *'Between the rhubarb plants… were parsley, chives, basil, thyme, sage, marjoram, anise and dill. I put parsley in everything but ice cream, Bob said, but even he admitted that tomato sauce, stew, kidney sauté, spaghetti or meat pie seemed tasteless without fresh basil once you had tasted them cooked with it.'*

MacDonald was not to know that some 60 years later parsley ice cream would be considered a gourmet delicacy.

It is a curious anomaly that the British twin passions for both gardening and cookery have not coincided to produce gardens stuffed with culinary herbs. As our interest in self-sufficiency grows, we are taking on allotments, keeping chickens and fretting over the provenance of our food. Yet vast numbers of us still regularly buy neat little cellophane-wrapped packets of fresh herbs from the supermarket (that is, when they have what we want in stock), without ever thinking to plant the very same plants in the garden so that we have a permanent supply. There should not be a garden or window box in the land that isn't home to some of the most basic culinary herbs – after all, you might buy herbs for a special meal, but will you buy three separate packets simply to flavour a stew? Buying fresh herbs is an unnecessary expense when most of us could buy the plant for the garden at very little extra cost or a packet of seeds at a fraction of the cost.

GROW YOUR OWN

Herbs are deliciously easy to grow and are, without exception, beautiful plants that contribute much to any garden design. In growing herbs you can take the moral high ground, for not only will your garden be fragrant and beautiful, it will be practical and functional to boot. In taking the plunge to grow a diverse range of aromatic plants you will find your use of herbs in the kitchen will multiply and your family's appreciation of your culinary endeavours will grow tenfold. It has taken me far too many years to discover the twofold secret of cooking good food: first and foremost, don't wander out into the garden and forget that you have a steak in the pan; secondly, have a plentiful supply of fresh herbs on hand to use on a daily basis.

This book contains information on 40 of the most popular culinary herbs. It tells you how to use them, what they taste like and how to grow them. It also has a few words on the medicinal properties of these culinary favourites. The focus is on beautiful plants that you will want to cultivate in your garden – I have omitted many of the delicious wild herbs, such as broom, that proliferate in the countryside. Information on these can be found in *Wild Food*, another book in this series (see Further Reading, page 94).

Once you expand your range beyond the basics you will quickly discover the subtleties of flavour that some of the more unusual herbs or exotic varieties can offer. Experience will encourage you to experiment. In her book *Une Soupe aux Herbes Sauvages*, Emilie Carles describes collecting plants in her native south-eastern France:

> *'I make good use of my walk gathering the plants I will need for my soup of wild herbs... This one is rib grass, and over there wild sorrel, tall drouille with its broad smooth leaves, nettle or salsify, sedge, yarrow, chalabréi with its broadly scalloped leaves and white flowers, tetragonia or wild spinach, some langue bogne of the light pink flowers and slim bright green leaves, a sage leaf and a sprig of chive. Then I add a touch of garlic, a few potatoes or a handful of rice and I get a rich and delicious soup. To make it come out right you have to watch the proportions. Not more than a bit of each herb is required; no single one should stand out – too bitter, too acid or too bland. Such is my wild herb soup.'*

There are few of us blessed to live in an area where wild herbs can be plucked at will with such confidence and ease. So on the following page is a recipe for herb soup that uses cultivated herbs and while it may be a little less poetic in tone – popping into the garden with a pair of scissors just doesn't strike the same note – I can guarantee it will be equally delicious and invigorating.

HERB SOUP

Use any combination of garden herbs: chives (see below of illustration), chervil, lovage, mint, parsley, sage, tarragon, thyme, rosemary, sorrel or whatever you have to hand.

25g (1oz) of butter
6 spring onions, sliced
175g (6oz) of potatoes, diced
1 clove of garlic
150g (5oz) of spinach
425ml (15fl oz) of vegetable stock
150ml (5fl oz) of single cream
2 tablespoons of chopped fresh herbs
Salt and black pepper
Lemon juice

Melt the butter and add the spring onions and the diced potato and cook gently to soften the vegetables. Add the garlic and spinach and stir. Then add the stock. Simmer and cook until the potatoes are soft. Pour this mix into a blender and blend until smooth. Return to a clean pan, add the cream and the herbs and warm through. Taste and add seasoning and the lemon juice.

THE HISTORY OF HERBS

The power of herbs has been harnessed by Man for thousands of years. Herbs were found in the grave of a Neanderthal man in Shanidar Cave in Iraq. They have been utilised by all religions, with many mentions in the Bible, the Koran and the Torah. They feature in folklore and legend across the world and throughout the history of Man.

Early hunter-gatherers collected herbs, but finding out what could safely be eaten would have been a matter of trial and error, with knowledge accumulated and passed down through the generations by word of mouth. The properties of these herbs would not have been scientifically understood; a seed or leaf that produced a hallucinogenic effect would have been subject to fanciful explanations and superstitions.

Herbs were so significant in Man's everyday life that they feature in the earliest texts. Their characteristics and uses as food, medicine, cosmetics, disinfectants, dyes and perfumes were recorded. They also played a significant part in some religious ceremonies and in the embalming process. One of the earliest Chinese herbals, the *Canon of Herbs*, detailed 252 herbal medications. It was attributed to the emperor Shen Nong who lived around 3000BC.

The Egyptians, the Romans and the Greeks were all enthusiastic herb users. Hippocrates wrote about the value of herbs in providing relief from pain and the historian Herodotus described 700 plants in common use back in 500BC. The Romans were responsible for introducing their favourite herbs to all parts of their conquered territories and are known to have brought some 200 Mediterranean species to the UK, including those culinary classics parsley, sage, rosemary and thyme.

Religion – notably the spread of Roman Catholicism – was significant in the development of herb gardens and the use of plants for medicines. The monastic movement originated in Europe where certain converts felt that a full Christian lifestyle was incompatible with secular life. They withdrew from the world, erecting high walls around their communities and creating a cloistered lifestyle, within which they were self-sufficient. Working for the poor and sick in the outside community improved their knowledge of herbs, the source of which is believed to have been *Materia Medica*, the classic text produced in the 1st century AD by the Greek physician Dioscorides. He described the properties of more than 500 herbs and his writings became, in early terms, a standard textbook and a prototype for future works, and allowed the monks to develop their reputations as skilled physicians. Infirmary gardens became a feature in many monasteries, often inspired in design by the classic Persian four-square garden.

Medicine aside, herbs were commonly used to flavour food and as a source of digestive relief. This is significant when you consider the quality of the food being consumed, combined with poor hygiene and lack of refrigeration. Much of the food would have smelt and tasted rank: herbs could mask the stench and putrid flavour of rotting meat. Monasteries became known for the beers, wines and liqueurs they brewed, flavoured with herbs such as liquorice, aniseed and hyssop; they were designed to act as a digestive and were consumed during and after mealtimes.

The real development of herb gardens in the UK came about in the 15th and 16th centuries, a time of relative peace and security when the landed gentry could devote their wealth to improving their grand houses and estates. Knot gardens were popular and often featured herbs, though their design was principally ornamental rather than functional. It was in the kitchen gardens of both nobility and peasantry that herbs were grown for culinary and medicinal purposes.

THE EARLIEST HERBALS

The first herbal, *Naturalis Historia* – essentially a dictionary of drugs – was produced by the Roman writer Pliny the Elder in 77AD. It expounded the original concept of the Doctrine of Signatures, the theory that the appearance and characteristics of a plant give clues to its use. The Swiss physician Paracelsus, who published a herbal in 1570, also based his work on the theory, but the Doctrine of Signatures was not popularised until the early 17th century when the German mystic, Jacob Boehme, published *De Signatura Rerum*. This apparently unscientific and fanciful approach seems in certain instances to have some basis in fact; some of the plants listed do function precisely as Pliny suggested. Willow, for example, grows in cold and damp places and was proposed as a treatment for rheumatic complaints caused by cold and damp. We now know that willow is a source of salicylic acid and in 1899 a German chemist developed acetyl-salicylic acid from it – the basis of aspirin.

Many new works were published in the 16th and 17th centuries. William Turner (1510–68) was the first person to attempt to name and classify native British plants. John Gerard (1545–1612) produced his *Herbal* in 1597 and personally cultivated more than a thousand species in his garden. Following on from this, John Parkinson detailed some 3,000 species in his *Theatrum Botanicum* in 1629. Nicholas

Culpeper (1616–54) continued with *The English Physician* in 1652. It detailed his thoughts regarding the astrological aspects of plants as well as their medicinal properties, an approach that diminished his credibility. He brought about so many cures that doctors claimed that he was using witchcraft.

In 1569 a Spanish doctor, one Nicolàs Monardes, published the earliest known American herbal. He listed many of the plants taken out by the settlers, who relied on fast-growing nutritious plants such as Good King Henry, parsley and sorrel to restore their health after the arduous voyage. He also noted plants such as bergamot, which the Native Americans used to make a form of tea: red bergamot (*Monarda didyma*) is named after him.

HERBS IN THE HOME

In the 17th century women began to play a part in recording the uses of herbs. They kept stillroom books, which, for the first time, detailed herbal remedies and cures that had been passed down through generations. The books were kept by matriarchs with a lifetime's experience in dealing with all matters relating to family health (stillroom refers not to a quiet place, but to the room where the still was kept – an essential piece of household equipment for distilling spirits and floral waters). At the same time, plants were being properly classified and every university of note had a physic garden where botany and medicine were studied together – though by the 18th century these fields were separating into two different sciences.

Patterns of life were changing irrevocably and with the Industrial Revolution many people moved away from the country to the city. Old-fashioned remedies were not available if you did not have a garden and, little by little, plant wisdom was lost. This was a situation unique to Britain: in other countries the enthusiastic cultivation of herbs continued unabated, but Britain had to import dried herbs for both medicinal and culinary use. The quality was poor and the practice of using herbs in cooking fell out of favour.

In the 20th century scientists learned how to isolate and synthesise the chemical properties of a plant. For the first time it became possible to produce accurate doses of drugs that were readily available from the chemist. Even so, herbs were still used medicinally; during World War I old remedies were relied on because of acute shortages of medicine and food. Herbs were grown for their nutritional content, while soldiers in the trenches used garlic, thyme and moss to help them save lives when conventional treatments ran out. Lavender was gathered and its oil was used as a surgical antiseptic in field hospitals. Nettles, which are rich in vitamins, nutrients and iron, were given to wounded soldiers as a tonic. In 1931 Mrs M. Grieve published *A Modern Herbal*, which detailed more than a thousand plants and generated new interest in the subject.

HERBS IN COOKING

The culinary use of herbs runs parallel to their use in medicine. The Egyptians mention cooking with herbs, notably coriander, in writings from 1550BC. An early cookery book by the Roman gourmet Apicius lists many interesting herb combinations. The Crusaders travelled to the Holy Lands and developed a taste for local herbs such as rosemary, basil and coriander. In the 16th century one Thomas Tusser, a steward, produced an exhaustive reference book titled *Five Hundred Pointes of Good Husbandry*, which recommends the cultivation

of some 70 salad herbs and pot herbs in the kitchen garden –
the term vegetable did not come into use until the 19th
century. After the Great Fire of London, in 1666, Leadenhall
market was rebuilt and as well as selling meat and hides, as
before, a new market was opened, which sold herbs, roots
and fruit. Herbs did not have the allure of spices, which
were highly prized and fought over because they grew
only in distant tropical climates.

In 1675 one Hannah Wooley wrote what is generally
regarded as the first cookery book by a female author. *The
Gentlewoman's Companion* mixed etiquette with housekeeping
tips, medical prescriptions and recipes. Herbs featured in
remedies and in recipes for preserving both fruit and meat.
A later book, *The British Housewife* by Martha Bradley,
published in 1770, recommends the use of thyme and winter
savory in Beef Ragoo or parsley, marigold and sweet herbs in
a Barley Broth. The characteristics of French cuisine – simple,
well-cooked, seasonal food – were established in the 18th and
19th centuries when the gastronomic excesses of court life
were abandoned with the French Revolution. Wherever
possible, fruit, vegetables and salad ingredients were picked
fresh, and it is a school of cookery where a few well-chosen
culinary herbs make a world of difference to flavour.

In Britain, supplies of fresh herbs of were simply not
readily available and the Victorians learned to prefer their food
plain and bland. It is worth noting, however, that despite this
Victorian puritanical streak, Eliza Acton's *Modern Cookery for
Private Families*, published in 1845, promoted the use of
garlic in sauces and Mrs Beeton's 1861 *Book of Household
Management* recommended the use of garlic in a recipe for
Chicken Marengo, and suggested tying rosemary, basil and
thyme together to flavour oxtail soup. Food shortages during

the two World Wars and the industrialisation of food production did nothing to improve the quality of British food and our reputation as dreadful cooks was probably justifiable in post-war Britain.

POST-WAR COOKERY

Primrose Boyd and Patience Gray introduced English cooks to French everyday cooking with their book *Plat du Jour*, first published in 1957. It was considered the height of chic by London hostesses, but was superseded by the work of Elizabeth David and Jane Grigson. But since those days, herb use has been on the rise. Foreign travel and the influence of a new breed of cooks, such as Elizabeth David, have transformed the way we eat. They brought French and Italian cooking into British homes, though at the time many of the ingredients listed were unheard of and almost impossible to obtain. Sixty years on the picture is very different. A selection of fresh herbs is available from supermarkets or via the internet. We are educated in a broad range of food ingredients and cooking styles and yearn to control both the quality and the provenance of our food. Growing your own herbs is one of the easiest ways to transform your reputation as a cook and to enjoy the whole process of cooking. These plants take the effort out of cooking, for the simplest dishes taste the best when flavoured and cooked to perfection. Modern chefs use herbs freely for good reason: in sourcing unusual plants and flavours they tempt our palate and establish a reputation for culinary prowess in the process.

GROWING HERBS

Herbs are delightfully easy to grow; given the right conditions they will thrive. Take a little time to cultivate a suitable environment, remove weeds and improve drainage and your efforts will pay handsome dividends. Aside from the value of their perfume and flavour, herbs are beautiful plants: some are evergreen and can provide year-round structure in your garden; others are sturdy perennials that flower year in and year out; even the annuals can be obligingly fertile, self-seeding freely where they will. These fragrant plants tend toward subtlety in leaf form and flower colour that combine for an overwhelming sensual impact.

All plants benefit from soil that is cultivated and herbs are no exception. With some exceptions, most appreciate a good-quality, well-drained soil in a sunny situation.

START WITH THE SOIL

Soil is graded according to its sand, silt and clay content – the ratio and size of these particles affects the behaviour of the soil. All soils can be improved with manure, garden compost, lime and sand as required. Loam soils offer the perfect mix with around 10–25 per cent clay, a ratio that offers high fertility with good drainage and water retention.

Sandy soil is light and suits many herbs very well for it warms up quickly in the spring and is free draining. Incorporating organic matter will further improve nutrient content and moisture retention.

Chalk soil is light and powdery to the touch; like sand it warms up quickly in spring, is free draining and moderately fertile. The downside is that it is by nature alkaline, with a pH reading of over 7, and most herbs prefer a sweet soil with a neutral pH balance of around 6.5. It may be necessary to lower the pH balance by adding sulphur. This problem will be ongoing and the soil will naturally revert; you may be best advised to create a raised bed (see below) and import sweet soil. If you wish to test your soil, pH testing kits are available from garden centres and are easy to use.

Clay soils are sticky and heavy, they are slow to drain and slow to warm up in the spring. The structure is easily damaged and clay soils can become compacted if worked when wet. Herbs will grow in clay, but do best if sand, coarse grit and organic matter are incorporated annually. If planting Mediterranean herbs, throw some grit into the planting hole to improve drainage immediately around the plant.

A silt soil is silky to the touch, it is more fertile and moisture retentive than sandy soils, but is more easily damaged by compaction – many herbs thrive in it.

MAKING A RAISED BED

Raised beds are easy to construct and have the advantage of being easy to work. They can be made from railway sleepers, brick or timber. Fill the bottom third of the bed with coarse drainage, put a mix of soil and gravel in the middle section and, in the top third, a mix of topsoil and compost.

PREPARING THE SOIL

Herbs, like all plants, do best when they don't have to compete for moisture and nutrients. If a patch is very weedy it may be necessary to dig it over carefully and extract all pernicious perennial weed roots as you go. It is worth taking the time and trouble to do this thoroughly, as the smallest remaining sliver of weed root will only sprout and return to haunt you. Weeding aside, digging aerates the soil and enables you to incorporate grit and sand to improve drainage.

Be careful how you dispose of pernicious weeds: don't put the painstakingly extracted roots or seed heads on your compost heap; they may not be destroyed in the composting process. Instead, put them in a black bin bag and when they have rotted down to an evil-smelling gloop, then you can put them on the compost.

There is also another approach. Organic purists regard digging more than once every five years as an unnatural activity that disturbs the natural balance and structure of the soil. They argue that applying a mulch is a far more effective way of suppressing weeds; worms will incorporate organic matter laid on the surface of the soil and aerate it at the same time. Thick blanket mulches are very effective at clearing weeds, but they are absolutely not a quick cure all – allow at least a year.

Some herbs are notorious weeds – nettle and dandelion being prime examples – in fact, a weed is merely a plant growing in the wrong place.

FEEDING THE SOIL

The beauty of many herbs is that they will withstand neglect and will flourish in soil that is low in nutrients. However, some herbs, such as angelica and coriander demand a rich soil. Most will benefit from the addition of some compost or organic matter such as well-rotted horse manure or leaf mould. Some soils are hungrier than others; sandy soil will leach nutrients at an alarming rate and require more frequent feeding and conditioning. In general, herbs do not require supplementary feeds; this can result in overly lush growth that merely serves to attract pests and diseases.

Soil that is deficient in nitrogen (N), phosphorus (P) or potassium (K) can result in poor growth and yellowing of the leaves. Container-grown plants, in particular, suffer from lack of nitrogen, which results in spindly growth and poor foliage. Commercial fertilisers are available in various forms, or you can make your own. Comfrey (*Symphytum officinale*) and nettle (*Urtica dioica*) fertilisers are easy to make and both have a high nitrogen content. To make comfrey fertiliser take a large bucket with a lid and put in as many comfrey leaves as will fit; weigh down with stones, cover and leave for five to six weeks. Then draw off the brown syrupy liquid that has accrued. It will smell vile, but is terribly good for your plants. It's a high potassium feed that will need to be diluted 15:1 before use. Throw the sodden leaves on the compost heap when you have finished with them. Nettle fertiliser is made in the same way, but tear up the leaves before adding to bucket. Leave for four weeks and dilute with water 10:1.

While herbs are delightfully trouble free, their very fecundity ensures that their growth and spread will need to be checked. Mint is notorious for its propensity to invade a flower bed and see off all incumbents. Contain it by sinking it into the soil in a plastic pot, or a long pipe – with a minimum depth of 45cm (18in) – to curtail its roots. Other plants, such as sweet woodruff (which is delicious in a May punch), will need to have their growth checked: try lifting and dividing plants, then pot them up and give them to friends. Shrubby herbs such as lavender, rosemary and bay need regular pruning to check their growth, but do not cut into old woody growth.

STARTING YOUR COLLECTION

Beginning your collection of herbs can be done simply and easily by a visit to the local garden centre, but buying even a few plants can become an expensive business. Some herbs are simply not readily available and your only option may be to purchase seed or to take cuttings from an obliging friend. Plants grown from scratch always seem to be that bit more robust than anything that has been cosseted in a nursery.

Sowing seeds is easy. Give them the right set of conditions that stimulate germination – water, air, the correct temperature and occasionally light – and they will be only too happy to oblige and sprout. I am a lazy gardener and never, ever sow a seed indoors if it can withstand being sown directly into the ground. There is no fuss over transplanting and no problems with damping off (where seedlings keel over and die due to a water- or soil-borne fungus). A good many herbs will not tolerate being transplanted and therefore can only be sown directly into the ground where they are to flower.

GROWING FROM SEED

Prepare a seed bed by digging in organic matter in the autumn – or apply it as a mulch and allow the cold weather to break up the soil to make digging easier. Rake the soil thoroughly in the spring and mark out a seed drill 5–10mm (¼–½in) deep, using a line of string to keep it straight. Sow the seeds at a rate of 2–3 per 2.5cm (1in), then lightly cover the drill with soil using the back of a hoe or rake and firm gently. Thin seedlings as directed when they reach 5–10cm (2–4in) tall. It may seem wasteful, but if plants are overcrowded they become leggy and prone to disease, so be ruthless.

Some half-hardy or tender plants have to be sown indoors: basil and marjoram are prime examples. Scatter the seeds on top of a pot of sterile seed compost and cover them lightly with sieved compost or perlite, if appropriate. Follow the instructions on the seed packet as some seeds need light to germinate – very few seeds can germinate in complete darkness. Stand the pot in water until the surface of the compost is damp – this is better than watering from above – then move to a window sill or propagator. Monitor pots carefully; they must not become too dry or waterlogged.

Prick out seedlings when they are large enough to handle and transfer them to a bigger pot. Keep them in a warm environment until they grow on, then start to harden them off – place them outside in daylight for increasing amounts of time, eventually graduating to a cold frame overnight, so that they can become acclimatised. Plant out after a couple of weeks. Don't be tempted to sow seed too early in the season or the seedlings will grow leggy and weak before the weather improves sufficiently to allow you to harden them off and plant them out.

TAKING CUTTINGS

Taking cuttings is an easy and effective way to increase your stock and it is far less of a fuss than growing from seed. There are four different types of cuttings: softwood, greenwood or semi-ripe, hardwood and root. It is essential to use a sharp knife – using scissors will only seal the end of the stem and discourage root growth. Stick to this rule and more of your cuttings will grow successfully. Some gardeners advocate the use of a hormone root powder to encourage root development, but many cuttings will take without any such assistance.

SOFTWOOD CUTTINGS are taken from the tips of new shoots, just below a node (leaf joint) in spring. Remove leaves from the bottom third of the cutting. The young material will root easily, but is very susceptible to moisture loss, so it is best kept in controlled conditions such as a greenhouse, cool house or propagator. Spray the leaves frequently with water in hot, dry weather. Rooting should take place in two to four weeks. This method of cutting is suitable for lavender, marjoram, mint, rosemary, sage, tarragon and thyme.

GREENWOOD OR SEMI-RIPE CUTTINGS are taken from mid-summer to mid-autumn from green wood just below a node. Remove leaves from the bottom third of the cutting. Place in a cold greenhouse or cold frame. These take longer to root than softwood cuttings, around four to six weeks, but are stronger and more resilient. Leave them until spring, then harden off. Greenwood cuttings are suitable for shrubby herbs such as juniper, lavender, rosemary and thyme.

HARDWOOD CUTTINGS are taken from mature hardwood at the end of the growing season, at any time between autumn and spring. Trim to just below a node and remove leaves from the bottom third of the cutting. Keep in a cold frame or greenhouse over winter. They are easy to maintain, but slow to root; the whole process can take a year and is used infrequently on woody plants such as elder and honeysuckle.

ROOT CUTTINGS are taken from strong and healthy roots when the plant is dormant – usually between autumn and spring. Dig up the plant and cut off 5–10cm (2–4in) sections of root that contain a growing bud. Place the root sections in a pot of compost and cover with a further 2.5cm (1in) of compost. This is a very easy method of propagation, especially suited to plants with spreading root systems such as mint.

Many plants thrive on being lifted and divided every few years; this checks their spread and encourages fresh growth. Division is best undertaken when the plant is dormant, in autumn or early spring. Simply dig up the plant and gently split it into two – or more – plants. Replant immediately and water well. Chives, thyme, lovage, oregano and marjoram are good candidates for division.

Layering is another gloriously easy method of propagation; it involves encouraging root development on a portion of a plant while it is still attached to the parent plant. In spring, trim leaves and side shoots from a healthy branch 10–50cm (4–20in) from the growing tip. Bring the stem down into the soil and peg it into place so that the growing tip is vertical. If the soil is poor you could add some compost and grit to assist the process. Keep the growing tip well watered. The following autumn, separate the new plant from its parent, but let it remain where it is for a full year to take root, after which time it can be transplanted. This is the best method to propagate bay.

PESTS AND DISEASES

Most herbs are naturally resistant to many pests and diseases; their aromatic fragrance seems to act as a form of insect repellent. However, in some cases this can also act as an attractant, tempting pests away from a main crop, which is why herbs like borage, chives, fennel, garlic, horseradish, hyssop and thyme are often grown alongside fruit and vegetables as companion plants.

Leafier herbs and young seedlings kept in the greenhouse will be more susceptible to attack, but good gardening practice helps to prevent problems from occurring. Clear away garden rubbish, pick off diseased leaves as soon as they appear and remove any visible pests. Avoid over-watering seedlings and young plants.

TOPIARY WITH HERBS

A number of herbs are good candidates for topiary, notably box, bay, rosemary and, less conventionally, lavender. It is very easy to train a plant into a ball or pyramid shape, but you need to be patient as it takes several years. I have a variegated box ball that I have been bringing on from a small sprig for the past ten years and it is still not a full, fat globe. The theory is simple: let your shrub grow until it is around 20cm (8in) taller than the desired finished height. Clip out the growing tip and remove all side shoots below the finished height. Prune the top shots lightly back to three or four leaves to encourage bushy growth and to tease slowly the plant into its desired shape. Keep repeating this process of trimming back as required to maintain shape (around 2–3 times a year) but allow the plant to grow a little larger and bushier each time.

Twisted bays, where the stem grows into a spiral, are beautiful structural plants; I have one that is my pride and joy and a focal point in the garden. To create one, start with a young plant and stake it with a 5cm (2in) diameter post. Select the strongest green stem and twist it around the post, stripping off side shoots. Train it upwards until it reaches the desired height and then allow the standard head to develop. It will take around 12–15 years for the stem to support the plant without a stake.

To create a standard bay with a plaited stem, take a young plant at least 30cm (12in) tall. Select three young green stems,

plait them and stake them for support. Allow the plant
to grow upwards, but strip away any side shoots. When
it has reached the desired height, allow the standard head to
develop. The stems will slowly grow and thicken to produce
the sculpted plait effect. It will take around ten years to look
fully mature.

HEDGING PLANTS

Box, lavender, rosemary, santolina and yew are all good
candidates for herb hedges of various heights – see the table
below for more precise information. They can provide shelter
from the wind, or simply serve as decorative dividers within
the herb garden. The key to establishing a good-looking hedge
is to ensure that it is wider at the base than it is at the top. For
the perfect cut, run a line of string at the desired height to act
as a guide for your shears.

Plant	Spacing	Height	Cut
Box	30cm (12in)	30–60cm (1–2ft)	2–3 times in the growing season
Lavender	30cm (12in)	60–100cm (2–3ft)	After flowering
Rosemary	45cm (18in)	1–2m (3–6ft)	After flowering
Santolina	30cm (12in)	60cm (2ft)	2–3 times in the growing season
Yew	60cm (2ft)	1.2–6m (4–20ft)	Twice yearly in summer and autumn

HARVESTING AND STORING HERBS

Growing herbs is a seasonal business and while most are best used fresh, there will be times of the year when plants are no longer useful, or even available. The solution is to find some means of preserving herbs so that you can continue to utilise their wonderful array of flavours without having to resort to raiding the supermarket shelves. And heaven knows this is not the most reliable source – if your whole dinner-party recipe revolves around a bunch of mint, you can guarantee it will be the one ingredient you can't find.

There are a few herbs that actually taste better dried than fresh; many can be frozen, or you can capture the essence of their flavour in oils and vinegars. The techniques are simple enough, but the key to success is knowing when to harvest – right down to the best time of day – and how to store your produce so that its flavours are properly preserved.

HARVESTING HERBS

GATHERING LEAVES

In general, the flavour of all leaf herbs is at its peak before the plant starts flowering. If you are planning on drying or freezing leaves, they should be picked before this stage has been reached. The youngest and freshest leaves are always the sweetest flavoured and the most succulent – older leaves can become unpleasantly bitter. It is best to collect leaves as early in the day as possible before the sun has dispersed the volatile oil, but *not* before all the dew on the plant has evaporated. Pick clean leaves that do not require washing or you will defeat the purpose of picking them dry. They can be wiped gently to remove any dust. Discard any leaves that look withered or diseased or which have been attacked by pests. For drying techniques see page 30. When cooking with fresh herbs, wash them only when you are ready to use them – excess moisture shortens their shelf life. If you are not using them immediately store them in the refrigerator, wrapped in a little kitchen paper and popped into an open plastic bag. Use a sharp knife to prepare them; you want to cut, not bruise your leaves.

PICKING FLOWERS

Flowers should be harvested at midday when they are fully open. Treat them with kid gloves. If you can't begin the drying process immediately, put them in a cool room for a short while to stop them wilting in the heat. If serving them fresh, young flowers can be delicious, with the possible exception of marjoram and basil – which are very strongly flavoured – and chive flowers, which are hard to eat. Try scattering a few over the top of a salad or fresh pasta – experiment with flavours.

COLLECTING SEED PODS

Seed pods should feel dry to the touch when harvesting, and timing is crucial: collect too early when the seed is green and it is likely to deteriorate. Pods generally turn from green to beige to brown or black as they dry. Leave collection too late and you may find the seeds have already dispersed. Some seeds can be gathered straight from the plant simply by shaking the seed heads into a paper bag. Otherwise gather the whole seed head.

Herb roots are at their most potent in the autumn after the plant has died back. Annuals can be dug up after flowering has ceased; perennials should not be dug up until the herb has matured for two to three years. Clean the roots thoroughly before storing.

PRESERVING TECHNIQUES

FREEZING

Freezing is a very simple method of preserving many herbs and should be done as routinely as freezing a glut of soft fruit from the garden. Prepare the herbs by ensuring they are clean. Remove leaves from stems, or flowers from stalks, discarding anything that is diseased or dirty. Divide the herbs up into the kind of quantities you use on a frequent basis, pop them into plastic bags and label. What could be simpler? You can also freeze ready-prepared portions of herb mixes such as *fines herbes* or *bouquet garni*. Herbs can be frozen in ice-cube trays: pop a teaspoon of the herb into the individual cell, pour water on top and freeze.

DRYING

There are very few herbs that taste better dried – in fact bay and oregano are the only ones – but it can be incredibly useful to have small quantities of your own freshly dried herbs, the culinary classics, for use in emergencies. These herbs should be infinitely superior in quality to the ones from the supermarket that have lodged at the back of the cupboard for years and are way past their best-by date. Dried herbs have a shelf life of just six months – after that date their flavour will fade. It is important to remember that dried herbs can be three to four times stronger in flavour than fresh herbs, so adjust quantities accordingly.

The romantic image of drying herbs is of picturesque bunches suspended from ancient beams. In fact this method will leave you with dirty, dusty herbs, coated in cooking fumes. Herbs are best dried in a warm and airy room, but direct sunlight should be avoided. Herbs deteriorate rapidly after cutting, so begin the drying process as soon as possible.

Evergreen or semi-evergreen herbs such as rosemary, sage, bay, thyme and lavender can be tied together in small bunches – no more than eight stalks to a bunch or the air will not be able to circulate. Cover them loosely with a paper bag to keep them clean and dust free, and hang them up dry in a cool, dark and relatively dust-free place – an airing cupboard or a loft could be ideal.

Feathery herbs such as fennel and chervil are best dried suspended as leafy stalks – remove the leaves when the drying process is complete.

EQUIPMENT

You will need to prepare a drying rack in advance. This can consist of muslin or cheesecloth stretched taut over a frame and stapled or tacked into place. Alternatively, you can use brown paper stretched over a frame, secured instead with masking tape and punched through with small holes. Larger-leaved herbs such as mint need to have the leaves stripped off and spread out on the drying rack. Flowers need to be laid out carefully on a muslin screen so that they will hold their shape.

Artificial heat does not assist the drying process; the herbs merely require a good circulation of air. If you are able to control room temperature then the ideal environment is as follows: for the first 24 hours a drying temperature of 32°C (90°F) is desirable; from then on the temperature should be reduced to 24–26°C (75–79°F). At this level herbs will take between four and seven days to dry, although thicker leaves may take a little longer. Leaves should feel brittle when dry – if they turn to powder they are too dry. Flowers take longer to dry – between one and three weeks. To store dried leaves and flowers place them in an airtight jar – first removing woody stems – and store away from direct sunlight. Use glass jars, not plastic containers, which would absorb the essential oils.

DRYING SEEDS

To collect seeds you can suspend the seed heads upside down and put a drying rack underneath to catch them. My preferred method is to tie a paper bag over the seed head; this will catch the seeds as they drop and stop them getting dusty. Seeds dry within about a fortnight in an airy room. For culinary use, store them in an airtight container, but for propagation purposes store them in a paper bag in a cool, dark place.

DRYING ROOTS

Roots should be washed carefully before drying and any top growth, fibrous offshoots and hairs removed. If roots are large it is a good idea to split them through the middle and cut them into smaller pieces to accelerate the drying process.

They can be dried in the oven: set the temperature to its lowest setting and turn the roots at intervals. Check regularly – when they break easily they are dry. Store them in airtight jars. If they become soft, discard them.

HERB OILS AND VINEGARS

If you want to give the appearance of a true gourmet, there is nothing like a few bottles of herb-flavoured oils and vinegars to set the right note. The fact is that a little trouble taken to create these aromatic dressings saves a lot of work later – a drizzle of herb oil or vinegar trickled over a piece of meat produces a marinade in a moment. It is a lost art due for revival: in days gone by the kitchen of any cook worth her salt would feature these labour-saving flavourings.

MAKING HERB VINEGARS

The process is blissfully simple – mix about ten tablespoons of a gently pounded herb with 600ml (1 pint) of white wine vinegar or cider vinegar. Do not use malt vinegar because its powerful flavour would dominate. Add the vinegar to the herb a little at a time; some cooks advocate warming the vinegar first. Pour the mixture into sterilised bottles and leave to steep – it will be ready to use in six weeks. Strain through a piece of muslin and taste; if it is too strong dilute with more vinegar. Before sealing the bottle add a fresh sprig of the herb for identification purposes. Tarragon vinegar makes a fabulous salad dressing and horseradish vinegar is great with cold meats. Basil, dill, garlic, chervil, rosemary, marjoram, mint, thyme and savory all make splendid herb vinegars, or they can be combined together in one bottle to make a mix, such as *fines herbes*. Coriander, dill

and fennel seeds also produce delicious vinegars, but add these
in the proportions of two tablespoons of lightly crushed seeds
to 600ml (1 pint) vinegar. Keep vinegars in a dark cupboard
to preserve their colour. Use within six months.

MAKING HERB OILS

Herb oils are incredibly useful in the kitchen, but don't go crazy,
just make a few oils with the herbs you use most regularly.
Garlic, basil and *bouquet garni* oil are the most commonly used
flavours. Basil oil effectively harnesses the distinctive flavour of
this herb and is superb mixed in Mediterranean dishes and for
sprinkling over pasta and pizza. A good garlic oil can be a real
life saver if you are short of time; it enables you to produce
salad dressings, pasta dishes and stir fries in just a few
moments. A *bouquet garni* mix is useful for meat, fish and stews.

To make a herb oil, start with a bland base oil such as
sunflower, groundnut or a mild olive oil. Choose your herb:
tarragon, thyme, rosemary, fennel, marjoram, savory, basil and
sage all work well. Gently bruise enough herb sprigs to fill a
wide-necked bottle or jar. Cover with oil and seal with a
corrosive-proof top. Leave to stand for two weeks in a cool,
dark place, and shake once a day. Strain the oil and taste – if it
is not strong enough, repeat the process. When the oil is ready
decant it into a dark glass bottle and add a sprig of the herb
for identification purposes. Use within six months.

HERB BUTTERS

Everyone has heard of garlic bread, but why stop at garlic?
Many herbs can be combined with butter and used similarly.
Try herb butter on toast or hot bread, pop it onto fish or

steaks prior to grilling or melt it over cooked vegetables. To make herb butter, finely chop your herb of choice, cream the butter and then mix the two together. Try making parsley butter. Take 125g (4oz) of butter and cream until soft. Add 2 tablespoons of freshly chopped parsley, lemon juice to taste and a pinch of cayenne pepper. Beat together, shape the butter into a roll, wrap in greaseproof paper and place in the refrigerator to chill. It is delicious with fish, steak or egg.

HERB JELLIES

Herb jellies are things of beauty with a perfect flavour. They are, in essence, an apple jelly flavoured with herbs, mint being a traditional favourite. If you make your own you will find it has far more bite than its commercially prepared namesake. Sweet marjoram, tarragon, thyme, sage and lemon thyme all make splendid herb jellies to accompany meat and fish dishes. Rose and lavender make sweeter jellies.

HERB JELLY

2.3kg (5lb) of cooking apples or crab apples
A few sprigs of your chosen herb
1.2 litres (2 pints) of distilled vinegar
Sugar
6–8 tablespoons of freshly chopped
   parsley, thyme and mint (or 6 tablespoons
   of freshly chopped sage or 4 tablespoons
   of freshly chopped rosemary)

Roughly chop the apples without peeling or
coring – remove bruised or damaged parts.

Put the pieces into a large saucepan with 1.2 litres (2 pints) of water and the herb sprigs. Bring to the boil and simmer for 5 minutes or until soft and pulpy – stir to prevent sticking. Add the vinegar and boil for a further five minutes. Spoon the apple pulp into a jelly bag, or use chemist's muslin, and leave to strain into a large bowl for at least 12 hours. Discard the strained pulp. Measure the liquid and put it into a preserving pan with 450g (1lb) of sugar for each 600ml (1 pint). Heat gently and stir continually until the sugar has dissolved, then boil hard for ten minutes. To test whether it has set put a spoon of the jelly onto a chilled saucer; if the jelly wrinkles when you push it with your finger the setting point has been reached. Remove the pan from the heat, spoon out any scum and stir in the chopped herbs. Cool a little more and stir the jelly to ensure the herbs are well mixed through. Pour the jelly into warm, clean jam jars and cover with waxed discs. Cover with cellophane when cool. Use within six months.

CRYSTALLISED FLOWERS

These tiny works of art are surprisingly easy to make. White or blue-flowered borage, violet and primrose all make good candidates. The end result will only last for a day or two, so ideally make them the day before they are required. First add a pinch of salt to an egg white and beat it lightly without frothing it. Dip the freshly picked flowers into the egg white and then into a dish of caster sugar. Put them onto a wire tray covered with a sheet of baking parchment. Lay another sheet of greaseproof paper on top and pop them into a low oven overnight, leaving the door ajar. Alternatively, put them into the airing cupboard for 12–36 hours until dry. When ready, store in an airtight container until required.

A DIRECTORY OF HERBS

Herbs can be grown in a designated space or mixed in among the flower border. Many are native to Mediterranean regions and need plenty of sunshine. A herb defined as enjoying a sunny situation will relish a minimum of seven hours of sunshine a day and will thrive planted close to paths or in tiny gaps on terraces and paths. A plant described as enjoying semi-shade will be content with just three to four hours of sunshine a day.

ALEXANDERS, BLACK LOVAGE
(*Smyrnium olusatrum*)

Alexanders was a popular culinary herb for centuries but is seldom used today. Yet it has much culinary merit: all parts are edible; leaves and shoots taste like a blend of parsley and celery but with a perfumed top note. It is delicious with fish. Fresh young shoots can be eaten raw in salads or lightly cooked. The stronger-tasting mature stems can be added to soups, sauces and stews as flavouring. The dark brown seeds – which look almost black – are peppery to the taste and the roots can be par boiled or roasted, or combined with other root vegetables to produce a mixed mash. This tall plant can reach 1.5m (5ft) in height. It has glossy, bright green, serrated leaves that resemble those of angelica. The tall stems are topped by yellow-green flowers from mid-spring to early summer. I have never needed to cultivate this herb for it grows in abundance on waste ground, grassy banks and beside hedgerows all around us. Once you have identified the plant you will spot it everywhere. The black seeds are a particular giveaway.

PROPERTIES: A digestive, calmative, diuretic and laxative.

CULTIVATION: Alexanders is almost too easy to cultivate: it will spread happily throughout the garden, though it favours rich, moist soil in full sun. It is biennial, so sow seeds in autumn and transplant to final planting positions in spring.

ANGELICA (*Angelica archangelica*)

Angelica is a majestic herb, a beautiful giant in the flower border – it can reach an imposing 2.4m (8ft) in a single season – and a marvel in the kitchen (see colour section for illustration). The leaves and stems have a sweet, musky flavour. It reduces the acidity of fruit and can be used as a sweetening agent: pop stems and leaves in with apples, plums or rhubarb as you stew them and you can reduce the amount of sugar required by up to a quarter. Sophie Grigson advocates trying the young stems as a spring vegetable, lightly steamed or boiled and topped with a little butter. The seeds are used as flavouring in liqueurs such as Chartreuse.

PROPERTIES: Angelica is said to be useful in soothing digestive problems and is thought to relieve flatulence. It was once regarded as an important medicinal herb and was carried to ward off the plague. Crushed leaves placed in the car are reputed to ease travel sickness.

CULTIVATION: Angelica is a short-lived perennial, often best grown as a biennial. Sow the seed in good, rich, moist soil in shallow drills in early autumn where the plant is to flower – the seedlings do not enjoy being transplanted. Thin to leave a space of 1m (3ft) between plants. The young plants will die back over winter and re-emerge the following spring. The seed quickly loses viability so it is important to plant promptly.

Home-made crystallised angelica is an entirely different confection to the shop-bought variety and is delicious. Take some young stems, cut into short lengths then put in a pan and boil until tender – but not pulpy – which takes about ten minutes. Remove from the pan and put aside to cool; remove the outer skins when it can be handled. Put the stems in a shallow dish with an equivalent weight of sugar (use granulated sugar or golden granulated sugar) and leave for two days. Return the sugar and angelica to a pan – it will have formed a syrup – and simmer very gently for ten minutes. Leave the angelica on a wire rack to dry for a couple of days and then store in an airtight container.

BASIL (*Ocimum basilicum*)

Basil is an essential culinary herb in the modern cook's kitchen. It is a central herb in many pasta dishes and a vital ingredient in pesto. It mixes especially well with tomatoes and eggs. Its pungent, peppery flavour is said to intensify with cooking, so it should only be added to sauces at the last moment and tastes better torn rather than chopped. The leaves will transform a tomato salad and can be used to flavour oil and vinegar (see pages 33 and 34) – both make delicious salad dressings. There are numerous varieties, so it is worth trying out a few to see which flavour you prefer – three to five plants will allow you to use the leaves liberally all summer. Basil does not dry well and although it can be frozen, I have never found it to be very satisfactory. Try to keep supplies going by bringing some pots indoors for the winter. Basil has fragrant, bright green leaves with clear veins (see colour section for illustration).

PROPERTIES: Basil is said to have sedative, digestive and antispasmodic properties and may be used to ease migraines.

CULTIVATION: Basil is a tender annual or, in warm climates, a short-lived perennial. It needs warmth, so should be grown in a sunny spot in well-drained, fertile soil. It is usually grown as an annual from seed. Sow in pots in early spring and keep under glass. Transplant into the herb bed when all danger of frost has passed and water regularly. Alternatively, sow directly into the herb bed in late spring or early summer. Pinch out flowering tops to encourage leafy growth.

PUTTANESCA

This is a classic Italian pasta sauce, a perfect background for vibrant basil and oregano.

Extra-virgin olive oil
3 garlic cloves
1 fresh red chilli, deseeded and chopped
2 teaspoons of fresh oregano or 1 teaspoon dried
2 x 400g (14oz) cans of chopped tomatoes
110g (4oz) of black olives, chopped
1 tablespoon of capers
1 can of anchovy fillets, drained
1 bunch of basil

Fry the garlic, chilli and oregano in the olive oil gently until softened. Add the tomatoes and simmer, then add the olives, capers and anchovies. Cook for 15–20 minutes until the sauce has reduced. When it is cooked, rip up the basil, stir it in and serve with pasta.

BAY (*Laurus nobilis*)

Sweet bay, one of the best-known culinary herbs, has aromatic and pungent leaves and no kitchen – or garden – should be without a bay tree. The leaves feature in many slow-cooked dishes, any number of stews, soups and sauces – notably béchamel – and in many milk-based desserts. Along with parsley and thyme it forms the central flavour of the classic *bouquet garni* herb mix.

Unlike most other herbs, bay leaves benefit from drying, which removes a hint of bitterness. Though picking sprigs a few days in advance will suffice, some serious cooks advocate using only the fully dried leaf for a superior flavour. To dry, hang up sprays of leaves in a dark, well-ventilated room – darkness helps to preserve their colour – until they are brittle. Strip the leaves and store them in an airtight container – again in darkness. Bay, an evergreen, has glossy, dark green leaves and insignificant yellow flowers in early summer; these are followed by black berries (see colour section for illustration).

PROPERTIES: This much-loved culinary herb is edible, but all other laurels are poisonous, so make sure that you have the correct species. An infusion of the leaves can aid digestion and stimulate the appetite.

CULTIVATION: Bay is a common garden plant that enjoys a sunny, sheltered spot and appears to be tough as old boots, but it can be tender in its first few years. Its shallow roots make it vulnerable to frost damage, and cold weather and strong winds can scorch the leaves. It is not the easiest of plants to propagate: layering in spring is the most efficient way. Cuttings require a lot of patience, a heated propagator and good humidity. Seeds are problematic because germination can take as long as six months. However, there is a ready supply of plants in garden centres, many clipped into formal shapes. One plant allowed to grow unchecked – it can reach 7m (23ft) – will more than take care of all your culinary demands.

CHICKEN WITH RED WINE AND BAY

This is simple, but delicious. Use the best chicken you can buy and a good, full-bodied red wine.

2 chickens, jointed into 8 pieces and scored
8–10 tablespoons of olive oil
12 bay leaves
3 whole heads of garlic broken into cloves, skins left on
¾ bottle of red wine

Heat the olive oil in a heavy-bottomed pan, place the chicken in the pan, season well and cook on both sides until golden brown – this will take around 10–15 minutes. Add the bay leaves, the garlic and the red wine and cook for 20–25 minutes uncovered, turning occasionally, until the wine has reduced by a third. Serve with crusty bread and a green salad.

BORAGE (*Borago officinalis*)

Borage is a pretty herb with starry blue or white flowers that appear from summer to autumn. The leaves and stem are green but covered with stiff white hairs (see colour section for illustration). Both flowers and leaves have a taste that is reminiscent of cucumber and are tasty chopped and tossed in a salad, or in a jug of Pimm's – the hairs seem to dissolve in the mouth. The flowers make a pretty garnish for any dish.

PROPERTIES: In ancient times borage was believed to have a strong impact on the body, inducing a sense of well-being, instilling courage and dispelling despair. Modern research has shown that it works on the adrenal gland, which affects the body's response in a crisis, which may explain its reputation. It is not advisable to use excessive quantities over long periods.

CULTIVATION: Borage will self-seed happily on any sunny site with well-drained soil. It does not like being transplanted, so sow seeds directly into the planting position and thin to 30cm (12in) intervals. Bees are attracted to its flowers, making it a useful companion plant for fruit and vegetables that rely on insect pollination, notably runner beans and strawberries.

CARAWAY (*Carum carvi*)

Caraway has been used as a herb since the Stone Age; seed has been found among the remains of Neolithic meals and in Egyptian tombs. On special occasions the Elizabethans served up the seeds with roast apples as the grand finale to a meal. It features in many traditional German, Austrian and Scandinavian dishes, including Sauerkraut. Caraway cake became a tea-time favourite in the court of Queen Victoria. This aromatic plant has bright green feathery foliage and in its second year it produces small umbels of white or pink flowers from early to mid-summer, followed by seed. The seed has a warm and spicy flavour with a hint of liquorice and is delicious in cakes, breads and soups. Try using it when you cook with apples. Caraway leaves can be chopped into salads and soups and are faintly reminiscent of a warm parsley flavour; the roots can also be cooked and eaten, and taste somewhat like parsnip.

PROPERTIES: In common with fennel, dill and anise, caraway is believed to have digestive properties; chewing the seeds is said to aid digestion, sooth flatulence, ease colic in babies and sweeten the breath.

CULTIVATION: Caraway is a hardy biennial that is easy to grow from seed. Sow it in autumn where it is to flower, for it does not tolerate being transplanted. Thin seedlings to 20cm (8in) intervals. It is equally content in sun or partial shade and will self-seed readily given the right conditions. Harvest seed heads in mid to late summer before the seeds begin to fall. Hang the heads upside down in a dry, well-ventilated place with a paper bag tied over the head or place a drying rack below to catch the tiny seeds.

CARAWAY-SEED CAKE

225g (8oz) of butter
225g (8oz) of golden caster sugar
4 large eggs
1 teaspoon of vanilla extract
2 level teaspoons of caraway seeds
225g (8oz) of plain flour

Heat the oven to 180°C, 350°F, gas mark 4 (reduce the temperature slightly for fan ovens). Grease a 20cm (8in) cake tin and line it with baking parchment. Cream the butter and sugar together until light and fluffy, then beat in the eggs one at a time. Add the vanilla extract and caraway seeds. Fold in the flour and put the mixture into the cake tin. Bake for an hour, or until a skewer inserted into the cake comes out clean. Allow the cake to cool a little before turning it out onto a wire tray.

CHERVIL (*Anthriscus cerefolium*)

Chervil should be grown in every garden for it is an indispensable herb that cannot be bought fresh. As a fringe benefit it is a tremendously pretty plant with bright green lacy fern-like leaves and white flowers that bloom in small umbels from early summer onwards. The downy leaf has a delicate, almost perfumed, sweet, parsley-like flavour allied with the merest hint of aniseed. As one of the *fines herbes*, along with parsley, tarragon and chives, chervil is a culinary essential and is best used fresh and in season; it does not dry successfully but can be frozen. It is delicious with eggs, cream cheese, fish, chicken and in sauces and soup – but do not add it until the last moment as it loses its subtle flavour if cooked for any length of time. Some people relish it chopped into salads. It is one of the Lenten herbs and chervil soup was traditionally consumed on Maundy Thursday.

PROPERTIES: The herb contains vitamin C, iron, carotene and magnesium. It is said to aid good digestion, reduce high blood pressure and act as a mild diuretic.

CULTIVATION: Chervil, unlike many herbs, grows best in moist soil in semi-shade – once the right spot has been found it will self seed freely. It does not tolerate being transplanted, so is best sown where it is to grow in shallow drills – thin seedlings to 20cm (8in). Sow at intervals throughout the growing season. It often does well sown between some of the giants of the flower beds where it can bask in their shadow and is happy in a container in the garden. It does not do well indoors, though it can cope with a greenhouse in winter.

CHICORY (*Cichorium intybus*)

Chicory has been an important culinary and medicinal herb for centuries and was used by the Egyptians, the Greeks and the Romans. The leaves and root have a pleasantly bitter flavour and the chicons – the tight crowns of forced leaves – are commonly used in salads. The chicons can also be boiled until tender and served with a hollandaise sauce or can be quartered and roasted with beef tomatoes, mozzarella, cubes of pancetta and a little garlic. Mature roots have been commonly used as a coffee substitute and are still used as an additive in coffee, a practice designed to soften the drink's bitter edge. Chicory is a tall, hardy perennial that will reach around 1m (3ft) in height. The leaves resemble those of the dandelion in shape, as do the flowers, though they are a glorious sky blue (see colour section for illustration). The plant will flower for precisely five hours a day and while the actual timing varies according to latitude, the leaves consistently align with north.

PROPERTIES: Chicory acts as a gentle diuretic, which helps the body eliminate uric acid and can be helpful in the treatment of gout. It is said that a decoction made from the root can help to soothe the urinary tract and the liver, and may alleviate some of the discomfort associated with gallstones and kidney stones.

CULTIVATION: If you want to grow chicons, sow Belgian chicory in summer; lift the plants at around four months old; trim the roots and leaves then place the trimmed plant in a bucket for forcing. Pack with sand or sandy soil and bring into the house where it is warmer. Water, keep covered and the plant will produce tight, pale leaves – the chicons – that are ready for eating in around three weeks. The red-leaved chicory, radicchio, can be sown *in situ* in early summer and can be eaten without forcing and cut repeatedly.

CHIVES (*Allium schoenoprasum*)

Chives, members of the onion family, have the double advantage of being both blissfully easy to grow and useful herbs. The crisp, tubular, hollow leaves have a distinctive, but subtle, onion flavour and are a wonderful addition to salads, soups and egg dishes, notably omelettes and scrambled eggs. They can be mixed with cream cheese or butter and used as a topping for baked potatoes and are delicious added to mayonnaise and new potatoes, or to a rich mash. Once you have a clump it will keep on coming up every spring, year after year and will amiably tolerate repeated attacks with the scissors – though always leave 5cm (2in) for regrowth. Chives taste best before they flower in early summer (see colour section for illustration).

PROPERTIES: Chives contain vitamin C and some iron. Like garlic, they are thought to be mildly antifungal and antibiotic.

CULTIVATION: Chives will be happy in a sunny situation, but will grow in partial shade. In the right growing conditions they will self-seed freely and can become a bit of a nuisance. They grow from tiny bulbs and will reach around 30cm (12in) tall. Plant them close to the back door so you can easily pop out with the scissors to snip off some stems whenever required. Once the plant has flowered, the stems are not as tasty so I keep cutting off the flower heads to extend their life. Chives are useful grown among vegetables as companion plants to deter aphids.

SCONES WITH CHEESE AND CHIVES

If you feel like being naughty, try this savoury delight.

175g (6oz) of self-raising flour
½ teaspoon of mustard powder
Large pinch of salt
Pinch of cayenne pepper
25g (1oz) of butter
75g (3oz) of cheese – any will do
1 tablespoon of freshly chopped or snipped chives
1 large egg
2½ tablespoons of full-fat milk

Heat the oven to 220°C, 425°F, gas mark 7. Sift the flour into a large mixing bowl, then add the mustard, salt and cayenne pepper; mix, then rub in the butter until it is crumbly. Mix in the cheese and the chives. Beat the egg and the milk together, then add it to the dry ingredients, kneading until you have a dough. Roll out onto a lightly floured surface until it is around 2.5cm (1in) thick, then cut into rounds – you will probably only get 6 scones out of this mix. Put the scones on a baking tray and brush the top with the dregs of the milk/egg mix. Bake for 15–20 minutes until they are golden brown.

HERB OMELETTE

A herb omelette is one of the simplest and easiest dishes to make. The traditional *fines herbes* mix is 30g (1oz) each of chopped parsley and chervil, 16g (½oz) chopped chives and a couple of chopped tarragon leaves. Use 9–18 eggs (approximately three per person) according to taste.

Basil (*Ocimum basilicum*)

Coriander
(*Coriandrum sativum*)

Marjoram
(*Origanum vulgare*)

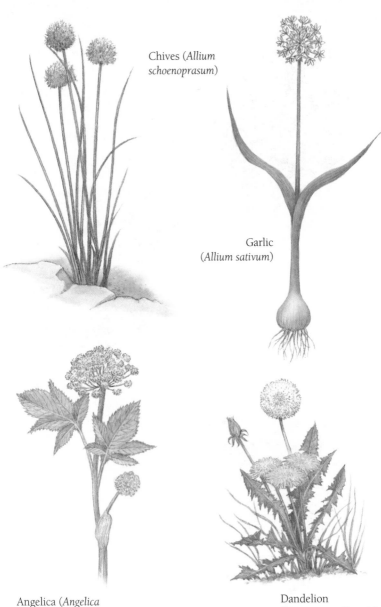

Chives (*Allium schoenoprasum*)

Garlic (*Allium sativum*)

Angelica (*Angelica archangelica*)

Dandelion (*Taraxacum officinale*)

Juniper (*Juniperus communis*)

Borage (*Borago officinalis*)

Bay (*Laurus nobilis*)

Crab apple (*Malus sylvestris*) with blossom

Wild strawberry (*Fragaria vesca*)

Spearmint or common mint (*Mentha spicata*)

Liquorice
(*Glycyrrhiza glabra*)

Lavender (*Lavandula angustifolia*)

Nasturtium
(*Tropaeolum majus*)

Rocket (*Eruca vesicaria*
subsp. *sativa*)

Summer savory
(*Satureja hortensis*)

Salad burnet
(*Sanguisorba minor*)

Sage (*Salvia officinalis*)

Chicory
(*Cichorium intybus*)

Scented-leaved geranium
(*Pelargonium graveolens*)

Rosemary (*Rosmarinus officinalis*)

Hyssop (*Hyssopus officinalis*)

Thyme (*Thymus vulgaris*)

Beat the eggs, add salt and pepper and the chopped herbs. Melt some butter in a pan and tip until the bottom and sides of the pan are coated. Add the mixture when the butter has just started to bubble, but before it begins to brown. When the edges have set, lift the omelette with a spatula so that the runny mix slips underneath to the heat. When it is just golden underneath and soft and creamy on top it is cooked. Serve and eat immediately – delicious with a salad and French bread.

CORIANDER (*Coriandrum sativum*)

Coriander is one of the most popular herbs all over the world and features in African, American, Indian, Latin American, Mediterranean, Middle Eastern and South-east Asian cuisine. It comes second only to parsley in supermarket sales figures for fresh herbs. The leaf looks somewhat like flat-leaved parsley (see colour section for illustration), but has a curious subtle perfume quite unlike that of any other herb. It has flat clusters of white flowers in early summer. Leaves and seeds have pungent, slightly peppery and quite distinct flavours. The name is derived from the Greek *koros*, which means insect, and is said to be so called because the plant smells like bedbugs. The leaves are heavily used in the cuisine of India and China and are a vital ingredient in guacamole, salsa and the spice mix *garam masala*. They can be added to soups, stews, sauces and curries or just sprinkled over grilled fish – especially tuna – meat or roast vegetables. The seeds are spicy and aromatic and can be added to soups and stews.

PROPERTIES: Coriander seeds are a digestive aid and act as a gentle diuretic. Coriander tea is said to ease nausea and flatulence as well as stimulating the appetite. The seeds are narcotic if consumed in large quantities.

CULTIVATION: Coriander is very easy to grow, though it does have the tendency to bolt – pick the leaves hard and snip off any flower heads to promote longevity. This half-hardy annual likes a sunny, well-drained site and is intolerant of damp conditions. Sow the seed *in situ* once all danger of frost has passed – it does not like the cold, or being transplanted. For a leaf crop, space plants at 5cm (2in) intervals; for a seed crop space at 23cm (9in). The leaves freeze quite well. Collect seeds when the smell of the plant alters and becomes more pleasant and when the seed heads change from green to brown. Unripe seeds taste frightful and will be unfit for use. Pick stems and hang upside down in a dry, airy place, in small bunches, with a paper bag over the heads to catch the seeds as they fall. Store them in an airtight container. Dig the roots up in the autumn – they have a subtle flavour and are used in Thai cuisine crushed into soups and curry pastes.

CHICKEN WITH CORIANDER AND GARLIC

My best pal Fiona Lovering is a demon cook and her favourite recipe is adapted from *The Moro Cookbook*. Cooked this way the chicken is very moist and tastes as good cold the next day.

1 chicken, around 1.5kg (just over 3lb)
2–3 heads of garlic
A little milk
30 saffron threads
1 bunch of coriander, roughly chopped
1½ level teaspoons of ground cumin
4 teaspoons of olive oil, plus extra
Sea salt and black pepper
Juice of ½ lemon

Preheat the oven to 220°C, 425°F, gas mark 7. Separate the heads of garlic into individual cloves. Put the cloves, in their skins, in a small saucepan and add milk to cover. Simmer for 25 minutes. Put the saffron in a cup and add 2–3 tablespoons of the hot milk. Drain the garlic and squeeze each clove out of their skins into a small bowl. Mash to a purée, then add the saffron and its milk, the coriander, cumin and olive oil and mix together. Season to taste. Ease the skin away from the chicken breast and thighs and push in the garlic mixture a little at a time. Put in as much stuffing as you can, but if you have any left, put it into the cavity. Season the outside of the chicken, and pour over the lemon juice and olive oil. Place in a roasting tin and cook for around an hour, basting occasionally. Check that it is cooked by piercing with a skewer; if juices run clear it is done. Leave in a warm place for ten minutes before serving.

CRAB APPLE (*Malus sylvestris*)

Crab apples are not easy to obtain, so grow your own or take note of where trees grow in the wild. The fruit is small and sour, but it has a unique delicacy and sharpness that no commercially grown fruit can compare with. Although not technically a herb, all parts of the crab apple can be used for its culinary, medicinal and other herbal qualities. Try roasting the fruit around a pork joint – they need about 30–45 minutes. Tree species vary in size and can reach 8m (26ft) in height. The pink, white or red flowers appear in profusion in late spring, and the conical orange and red fruits follow in early to mid-autumn (see colour section for illustration). Trees will produce a crop of around 9kg (20lb); store fruits wrapped in paper in a cool, airy place.

PROPERTIES: The pectin found in apples and crab apples is said to aid the elimination of toxins, stimulate digestion and help to balance cholesterol levels. Crab apple is also one of the original Bach flower remedies.

CULTIVATION: Crab apples appreciate a fertile, well-drained soil. Plant a tree in autumn with a good dressing of compost and ensure that it is well watered the following spring. Stake the tree and leave the stake in place for a couple of years until the tree is stable and well rooted. It does not need to be pruned, but crossing branches and dead wood should be removed; you might need to wear gloves because some varieties are thorny.

CRAB-APPLE JELLY

2.7kg (6lb) of crab apples
Preserving or golden granulated sugar

Wash the fruit, cut into quarters and place in a large pan. Add 1.7 litres (3 pints) of water, bring to the boil and simmer for 1½ hours or until the fruit is mushy – you may need to add a little more water in the cooking process. Strain the fruit through a muslin cloth – available from chemists – or jelly bag. Measure the extracted goo and return to the pan with 450g (1lb) of sugar for each 600ml (1 pint) of extract. Heat gently, stirring to dissolve the sugar, then bring to the boil and bubble until a set is obtained on testing – either when it reaches 105°C on a sugar thermometer or when a spoonful of jelly placed on a chilled saucer wrinkles when you push your finger through it. When setting point is reached, take the jelly off the heat. Remove any scum with a slotted spoon and pot the jelly into the warm, clean jam jars. Cover with waxed discs and seal with cellophane and a rubber band.

DANDELION (*Taraxacum officinale*)

If you sample a dandelion leaf plucked straight from the garden you will be spitting out the bitter greenery a few seconds later. Turning this common weed into something that tastes fabulous demands no small measure of commitment. First, the plant should be forced (grown early in the season in an unheated glasshouse), which removes some of the bitterness from the leaves. Then the leaves should be blanched (covered over with a pot) so that they grow pale and yellow. The result is an incredibly tasty leaf. These leaves are delicious in salads, notably with bacon. Victorian ladies favoured them in sandwiches, served with plenty of lemon and black pepper, and their full-flavoured gusto mixes well with bland food such as eggs and cream. You can try blending the leaves with spinach to bulk up quantities while retaining the taste. Dried dandelion roots used to be roasted, ground and used as a coffee substitute. The bright green, deeply toothed leaves rise from a basal rosette. The familiar yellow flowers appear from mid-spring to early autumn, and turn overnight into globular, fluffy seed heads (see colour section for illustration).

PROPERTIES: Dandelion is a strong diuretic and thought to be helpful in the treatment of liver complaints. It contains vitamin C, vitamin A and plenty of iron.

CULTIVATION: Cultivated varieties of dandelions have broader leaves and a less assertive flavour. For culinary purposes they should be regarded as annuals; sow the seeds in early spring and thin seedlings to 15cm (6in), with 30cm (12in) between rows. They require good, rich, moist soil; if they get too dry the leaves become more bitter. Cover with a pot, or tie-up the leaves for a minimum of seven days to blanch.

DILL (*Anethum graveolens*)

Dill is a tall plant with feathery bright green foliage. It carries
flat heads of yellow flowers from early to mid-summer, after
which the seeds appear; both leaves and seeds are used for
flavouring. It has a sharp, sweet taste that is often used with
fish; only add the leaves at the last moment as the distinctive
flavour is lost with cooking. Try adding the leaves to salads, or
mixing with sour cream. For glorious canapés, cut up pieces of
soda bread, whack a mix of crème fraîche and horseradish on
top (or settle for a smear of cream cheese), pop a little piece of
smoked salmon on top of that and finally add a sprig of dill. It's
also a delicious alternative to mint with new potatoes and is
fabulous with buttery broad beans or mushrooms. The flat
brown seeds, which split into two, have a warm, aromatic
flavour, faintly reminiscent of caraway. Dill is used to flavour
vinegar and pickles, notably pickled cucumbers. The herb
is heavily employed in Scandinavian cuisine and also in its
native Iran.

PROPERTIES: Dill has been used as a calmative for centuries;
the name derives from the Norse *dilla* or the Anglo-Saxon *dylle*
which mean 'to lull' or 'to soothe'. It is said to be particularly
effective in calming colic in babies and is the basis of gripe
water. Bruise a handful of seeds and steep in a glass of hot
water for an hour, give a teaspoon to the baby, or a tablespoon
to the nursing mother – who can treat the baby indirectly via
her milk. The seeds are rich in mineral salts and, used whole
or ground, can be a useful alternative to anyone following a
salt-free diet.

CULTIVATION: Dill appreciates well-drained soil in full sun.
It can be tricky to establish as it hates being transplanted, but

once it is in the right spot it will self-seed freely. Sow seed in drills where it is to flower from mid-spring to early summer. Thin seedlings to 23cm (9in) apart. Once the plant has flowered the leaf is of no use as a herb, as all energy goes into seed production. To keep a continual supply, sow seeds at fortnightly intervals. Do not plant it close to fennel as the plants cross pollinate and hybrid seed will result. To harvest seeds, pick the seed head and hang upside down in a warm, dry, room; tie a paper bag around the head to catch the seeds as they fall, then store in an airtight container.

STUFFED EGGS

This recipe comes from a Scandinavian acquaintance, Mia Haikonen; she always produces the dish with a flourish at parties, and very tasty it is too!

10 free-range eggs
Mayonnaise
2 cans of tuna
Salt and pepper
Dill

Cook the eggs in boiling water until hard boiled – around ten minutes. Cool in a bowl of cold water. Remove the shells and cut the eggs in half, removing the yolks with a small spoon as you go and placing them in a separate bowl. Add some mayonnaise and two cans of tuna to the egg yolks; mix and add salt and pepper to taste. Fill the eggs with the mixture and sprinkle chopped dill over the top.

FENNEL (*Foeniculum vulgare*)

Fennel is one of my favourite herbs: every part of it can be eaten and it has a wonderful aniseed fragrance. It is a welcome addition to the flower border with masses of delicate, feathery foliage and flat, sulphur-yellow flower heads. It flowers throughout summer and autumn and the plant increases in size and strength year after year. The herb is commonly associated with fish but is equally delicious with lamb. Try using the chopped leaves in stuffing for fatty meat such as pork and duck or try sprinkling chopped leaves over new potatoes. Sophie Grigson recommends using it in mayonnaise to go with poached chicken, but suggests that the foliage is blanched first for a few seconds to soften it up. Cut open fish and put a handful of fennel inside, or try sprinkling it over shellfish. Throw fennel and fennel seeds in with a ham as you boil it. The leaves have a much milder flavour than the seeds.

PROPERTIES: Fennel is said to help alleviate heartburn and constipation. It acts as a diuretic and is reputed to ease the symptoms of cystitis. A teaspoon of fennel tea is good for babies with colic, or the nursing mother can drink a cup of the tea instead. However, the tea should be drunk only in moderation. Chewing the seeds is said to reduce hunger pangs.

CULTIVATION: Theoretically fennel is very easy to grow, but it is picky about its situation and needs a sunny position in well-drained soil – it's not very happy on clay and you may need to add sand and grit to improve drainage. Given the right conditions it will flourish and self-seed. Sow seed directly into the ground when all danger of frost has passed; thin seedlings to 50cm (20in) intervals. It will grow in a container, but may need staking. Cut leaves as required; harvest seeds when they turn grey green, generally in early autumn. Cut the seed heads and hang upside down with a tray underneath to catch the seeds as they fall – or tie a large paper bag over the flower head. Don't grow fennel close to dill as the two plants will cross pollinate. It is a useful companion plant as it attracts masses of hoverflies which in turn feed on whitefly.

If you want to produce the edible bulbs you must grow Florence fennel. Prepare the ground in advance by digging in compost over the winter. Water the plants well and when the bulbs begin to swell, draw the earth up and around them as you would for potatoes. Harvest the stem bulbs in late summer.

GARLIC (*Allium sativum*)

Garlic has been used as a flavouring for many thousands of years. Its pungent aroma has made it an indispensable culinary herb the world over (see right and colour section for illustration). The raw clove has the strongest taste; just rubbing it around a salad bowl or over the skin of a chicken imparts a hint of its unmistakable tang. Cooking it with other ingredients mellows its impact, particularly when mixed with other robust items such as onions and tomatoes. Roasted in its skin its flavour changes again, becoming smoother and gentler. When poached it releases a whisper of flavour. Whole bulbs or cloves can be placed alongside meat when roasting, or slivers can be inserted into flesh – especially delicious in pork or lamb. Take care not to cook garlic in oil or fat that is too hot as this impairs the flavour.

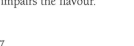

PROPERTIES: Garlic contains sulphur compounds – allicins and alliins – that are thought to help prevent cancer and cardiovascular disease. There is evidence that high garlic consumption is associated with low cancer incidence.

Garlic contains potassium and vitamin C. It is known to have antiseptic and antibiotic properties – antiseptic dressings soaked in garlic juice were routinely used in World War I.

CULTIVATION: Tradition holds that garlic should be planted on the shortest day of the year and harvested on the longest – in fact it can be planted in any well-drained soil in autumn, ideally before the first serious frosts set in, or as late as March. Plant cloves with the pointed end upwards, in a sunny position in rich soil, at a depth of 2.5cm (1in). Space cloves at 10cm (4in) intervals. Freshly harvested garlic is delicious, but it keeps quite well if hung in plaits somewhere cool and dry.

ROAST PORK BELLY

This recipe is adapted from *Ottolenghi: The Cookbook* and is just divine. I love pork belly: not only is it delicious, but reasonably priced too. It was difficult to decide which herb to file this recipe under, but the garlic is a must.

1 piece of pork belly, 2–3kg (4–6lb)
1 head of garlic, cloves peeled and crushed
2 tablespoons of thyme, chopped
2 tablespoons of rosemary, chopped
150ml (¼ pint) of olive oil
Coarse sea salt and black pepper
½ bottle of dry white wine

Heat the oven to 230°C, 450°F, gas mark 8. Put the garlic, herbs and olive oil in a food processor and purée. Put the pork belly in a roasting tin, skin side down, and season with salt and pepper. Then use your hands to rub the garlic mixture all over the top of the meat and press it down firmly. Turn the belly skin side up, wipe the skin dry with kitchen paper and sprinkle lightly with sea salt (don't use too much salt as it can prevent the crackling from forming). Roast for 20 minutes, then turn the oven down to 190°C, 375°F, gas mark 5 and cook for another 40 minutes. Turn the oven down to 170°C, 325°F, gas mark 3 and pour the white wine into the tray – but not over the skin. Roast for another hour – you may need to add a little more wine to keep the base of the tin moist. Finally, turn the oven down to 110°C, 225°F, gas mark ¼ and continue roasting for another hour until the skin is thoroughly dried and brittle. Remove the pork from the oven, leave to stand for 10 minutes, then use a sharp knife to cut it into segments.

AIOLI

4 cloves of garlic
¼ level teaspoon of salt
2 egg yolks
300ml (½ pint) olive oil
2 tablespoons of lemon juice

Crush the garlic with the salt using a pestle and mortar. Add the egg yolks and beat the mixture well. Add the oil, a drop at a time at first, beating to incorporate each addition until the mixture is thick and smooth. Add the lemon juice to taste.

HOP (*Humulus lupulus*)

Hop is an underrated herb most commonly associated with the brewing industry, which uses its flavouring and preserving qualities. It deserves to be planted in all gardens for it is an attractive plant that will scramble over all manner of unsightly objects. It has deeply lobed leaves, somewhat reminiscent of the grape vine, and bears male and female flowers on different plants. The male flowers are small and green, but the female flowers are larger and develop into the familiar green papery cones; these are the source of the resin that gives hops their distinctive fragrance, which has been likened to a rare combination of garlic, yeast and ripening apples. The new season's shoots can reach up to 7.5m (25ft) in height – they always twine in a clockwise direction – before dying back completely in autumn. The young side shoots can be cut off and eaten and are prized as a delicacy in Italy, France, Belgium and Germany. Cook them in lightly salted boiling water much like asparagus; they are delicious served with eggs.

PROPERTIES: Hops are said to be both a sedative and a soporific and were traditionally used to help nursing mothers boost milk production. Research has now shown that the herb contains a hormone which explains this therapeutic action. Pillows stuffed with hops are said to calm the nerves. Only female flowers are used for medicinal purposes.

CULTIVATION: Hops are very easy to grow; their main requirement is for support. The chief methods of propagation are root division in spring, or softwood cuttings taken in spring or early summer from established female plants. Thin out the young shoots in spring, but don't throw them away – eat them.

HORSERADISH (*Armoracia rusticana*)

Horseradish root packs the most incredible punch with a hot, sharp, biting, flavour. The plant has tall, architectural leaves that look like an elongated dock leaf. It self-seeds freely and once you have it in the lawn it is almost impossible to eradicate. The long, white, tapering, fleshy root contains oils similar to those in mustard: the strongest flavour comes from roots pulled in autumn; roots pulled in spring are much milder. They can be harvested at any time of the year, or they can be lifted and stored in autumn; cover them with sand and keep in a cool, dark place. The root must be peeled before use and then grated – you may want to wear glasses or goggles as the sap will sting horribly if it gets in your eyes. Horseradish sauce is a traditional accompaniment for roast beef in the UK; the Germans and the Danes use it more readily, as an alternative to mustard or mixed with stewed apples to accompany duck and goose. The flavour is lost when it is cooked so it should always be used raw. Fresh young leaves can be chopped and added to a salad.

PROPERTIES: The plant has antibiotic properties and was formerly associated with the treatment of urinary-tract infections and respiratory complaints. It is also an alarmingly powerful nasal decongestant. The root contains vitamin C, calcium, magnesium and sodium.

CULTIVATION: Horseradish enjoys a sunny situation and rich, moist soil. It is easy to propagate by division in the spring. It is widely found on wasteground and you can dig up a small piece of root without harming the plant. Only sow seeds with the greatest of caution – the resulting crop may take over your garden. Horseradish can be grown near potatoes as a companion plant to improve disease resistance.

Approximately 60g (2½oz) of fresh horseradish root
150ml (¼ pint) of double cream or sour cream
½ teaspoon of salt
½ teaspoon of pepper
2 teaspoons of white wine vinegar
1 teaspoon of white sugar
½ teaspoon of mustard powder (optional)

Peel and grate the horseradish. Whip the cream and fold in
the rest of the ingredients. Chill for two hours before serving
to allow the flavour to infuse. Nigella Lawson livens up her
horseradish with the addition of uncooked, grated beetroot –
very tasty and a fabulous shade of pink!

HYSSOP (*Hyssopus officinalis*)

Hyssop is an underrated fragrant herb that deserves much
wider recognition. The key is to have a fresh plant in the
garden – easy enough as it is a semi-evergreen shrub. Once
you have discovered what a delicious addition it makes to all
manner of dishes, you will wonder how you survived so long
without it. The leaves are warm and spicy with an edge of
bitterness faintly reminiscent of mint and rosemary and can
be picked throughout winter when many other herbs are not
available. Hyssop is tasty in game stews and is wonderful
mixed into stuffing as an accompaniment for rich and fatty
meat. In Gascony, hyssop is used in *bouquet garni*. Curiously
it is also rather splendid with fruit such as peaches and plums,
but you will need to add only the tiniest sprig in the cooking
process to scent the dessert – too much and it will overpower

the flavour of the fruit. Hyssop is reputed to be one of the significant flavouring herbs in the liqueur Chartreuse. It will grow to around 1m (3ft) if left unchecked. The aromatic, narrow, pointed dark green leaves grow on erect stems; blue, white or pink flowers are produced throughout the summer and attract bees (see colour section for illustration).

PROPERTIES: The herb has a variety of uses; it contains an essential oil whose medicinal action is similar to that of garden sage. It is said to aid digestion, soothe sore throats and assist in the treatment of urinary-tract infections. Hyssop is helpful in treating bruising in general and a black eye in particular. Crush a handful of leaves in a muslin cloth or clean handkerchief, dip in a bowl of boiled water and apply to the affected area as hot as you can bear it. Continue until the swelling starts to subside. Pregnant women should not use this herb.

CULTIVATION: Hyssop appreciates a sunny position in well-drained soil and makes a good container plant. Sow seed directly into the ground in spring and thin seedlings to 30cm (12in) intervals. It can also be propagated by taking stem cuttings in spring. Like lavender, hyssop can be used to edge borders and flowerbeds and can be clipped into shape, but it will need renewing around every five years.

JUNIPER (*Juniperus communis*)

Juniper berries have a clean, strong, tangy flavour – oil from the crushed berries is famously used to flavour gin. They are deliciously sharp with fish and bring a tang to casseroles using rich meat such as game, pork and venison. My favourite and most regular use is to throw a few berries in with cabbage, which transforms its taste. In marinades and sauces four juniper berries can be used to replace one bay leaf. It is vital when harvesting the berries that you check for ripeness – one bush can have fruit at different stages of ripening as they change gradually from green to blue-black over three years. Collect berries at the end of the summer and spread them out on a metal tray in a warm room, turning regularly. Allow them to shrivel and dry, which takes up to three weeks, then store in an airtight jar. This aromatic evergreen shrub or tree can reach an impressive 8m (26ft) in height. It has needle-like grey-green leaves and insignificant flowers in early summer (see below and colour section for illustration).

PROPERTIES: Juniper is a cleansing, eliminating and diuretic herb that has been used for centuries. It is said to be helpful in treating urinary-tract infections and in dealing with bronchial complaints. It should not, however, be used as a long-term treatment. Pregnant women must avoid it (some varieties have abortive properties), as should anyone with kidney problems.

CULTIVATION: Juniper likes an open situation in good garden soil. The berries do not germinate easily: sow them when ripe, in spring, in a cold frame and do not plant the seedlings out into the garden until they are two years old. Stem cuttings are more likely to be successful: take from new growth in autumn or spring and plant out the following season. Berries are produced on female plants only, but you will need a male plant nearby for pollination.

LAVENDER (*Lavandula angustifolia*)

Lavender is famous for its overwhelming perfume and was traditionally used to flavour jellies, ice cream, shortbread and custards. More adventurous cooks have been rediscovering the subtle nuances that its aromatic flavour can bring. The leaves are milder than the flowers and can be used when they are young and at their best – before the plant comes into flower. Try chopping them up and popping them into a salad. Leaves and flowers can be rubbed over a joint of meat, notably lamb, or try frying them very gently with a little garlic and using as a marinade for lamb or fish. Lavender jelly is delicious and can be served with scones or as an accompaniment to meat. As with the scented-leaved geranium, the flowers can be strewn across the base of a cake tin before the sponge mixture is poured in – remove the flowers when the cake is cooked, leaving a sponge infused with the perfume of lavender. This herb is a hardy evergreen subshrub; it has silvery grey foliage that ripens to green as it matures. The purple flowers are borne on tall, slender spikes and are intensely attractive to bees (see colour section for illustration). Dutch lavender (*Lavandula vera*) is reputed to be the best variety for culinary purposes.

PROPERTIES: In addition to its wonderful fragrance, lavender has antiseptic, disinfectant and calmative qualities. The oil is marvellously soothing when applied to stings and burns, and a few drops in the bath should help to induce restful sleep.

CULTIVATION: Lavender basks in a warm, sunny spot in fertile, well-drained soil. Some species are frost hardy, but if you live in a cold area you may be advised to grow the plant in a container and put it somewhere sheltered in winter. Plants can be propagated from softwood cuttings in spring, or semi-ripe cuttings in late summer or early autumn. Layering is another option and is best tackled in autumn. The plants do not last for more than three to five years before they become very woody. Prune them lightly in early autumn, remove flower spikes and a little of the annual growth, but take care not to cut into any old woody growth. For hedging, space plants at 23–30cm (9–12in) intervals.

LIQUORICE (*Glycyrrhiza glabra*)

The juice derived from the root of this herb provides the flavour for liquorice sweets. It contains glycyrrhiza, which is said to be 50 times sweeter than sugar, but the root also contains bitter substances that tone down the sweetness. It is this quality that has made it useful in confectionery and brewing. The flavour divides public opinion: you either love it or hate it! The root can be chewed when dried – it was a popular confection after World War II. Liquorice plants can reach an impressive 1.5m (5ft) in height; they have opposing grey-green leaves and bluish purple pea-like flowers that appear in the late summer, followed by red-brown seed pods (see colour section for illustration).

PROPERTIES: The herb is a renowned remedy for colds and chest infections and is still widely used in commercial cough remedies and throat sweets. It lowers acidity levels in the stomach, helping to relieve indigestion and heartburn. It is a mild laxative. Liquorice should be eaten in moderation: too much can raise blood pressure.

CULTIVATION: The plant does best in deep, rich soil and thrives in long, hot summers. It benefits from some protection from frost. Root division is the most effective means of

propagation. Lift and divide plants in early spring or autumn
when the plant is dormant. Ensure that there is one bud on
any piece of root – they can reach an impressive 1m (3ft) in
length so there might be some serious digging involved. Pot
up the roots in compost; water and keep in a warm place
until shoots appear. Harden off plants before planting out at
1m (3ft) intervals; they will take a couple of years to become
established. Roots can be harvested for drying when the plant
is three years old.

LIQUORICE ICE CREAM

This is adapted from a recipe by Heston Blumenthal. It
makes around 2 litres (3½ pints) of ice cream. You will need
an electric mixer, either free standing or a sturdy hand-held
mixer and a large bowl with a rounded base. You will also
need an ice-cream machine.

4–6 liquorice sticks
600ml (1 pint) of milk
10 coffee beans
12 level tablespoons of skimmed milk powder
6 egg yolks
120g (4oz) of caster sugar
Seeds scraped out of 1 vanilla pod

Cut the liquorice sticks into small pieces. Pour the milk into
a heavy-based saucepan with a minimum 1.5 litre (2½ pint)
capacity. Add the coffee beans, milk powder and liquorice.
Bring to the boil over a medium heat; the moment it comes to
the boil, turn down the heat and allow the mixture to simmer
for five minutes. Remove from the heat and leave to infuse for

20 minutes. Meanwhile, put the egg yolks, sugar and vanilla seeds into a mixer. Turn the machine to its top speed and beat until the mixture is very thich and white (this takes at least ten minutes). Place the pan back on the heat and return to a simmer. Gently pour this hot mixture into the egg mixture, beating all the while. Pour the mixture back into the pan, place over a very low heat and stir continuously with a wooden spoon until it thickens slightly. It is essential that the mixture does not boil or it will become grainy. The custard is ready when it coats the back of a spoon; lift the spoon out, hold horizontally and draw a line along its back with your finger – if the line keeps its shape, the custard is done. You will need a bowl ready to hold the custard; stand this in a larger bowl containing ice and a little cold water. Strain the custard through a fine sieve into the bowl and stir for a few minutes until the mixture is cold. Churn the custard in an ice cream machine. Store in a sealed container in the freezer. Remove from the freezer one to two hours before serving.

LOVAGE (*Levisticum officinale*)

Lovage was an important culinary herb for centuries but its use diminished. It tastes rather like a subtle, spicy and aromatic celery with a hint of musky lemon. It is an exceptional herb and well worth cultivating. It is good in stews, soups and casseroles but should be added with a light hand. Young stems can be eaten as a vegetable – cook them in lightly salted water until tender. The stems can also be candied like angelica and used to decorate pies and cakes. The seed can be added to mashed potato and boiled rice or sprinkled over home-made bread immediately before baking. The leaves can be used fresh or can be frozen, but should be

harvested before the plant comes into flower. Gather
seeds as seed heads start to turn brown; tie a paper bag
over their heads and hang upside down to dry. Lovage
is a tall, handsome plant that can grow to 2.1m (7ft)
in height. It carries aromatic toothed leaves on long
stems. Greenish yellow flowers appear in clusters from
early to mid-summer.

PROPERTIES: Lovage is reputed to stimulate the appetite
and aid digestion; it also acts as a diuretic. It should not
be used by pregnant women or anyone suffering from
kidney problems.

CULTIVATION: Lovage is a hardy perennial that likes a warm,
sunny spot, but also requires moist garden soil. It can easily
be propagated by division in spring, best undertaken just as
the leaves start to show. Plant the root sections at 60cm (2ft)
intervals towards the back of the border. Alternatively sow
seeds in a nursery bed, again in moist soil in sunshine, and
transfer to planting position in late autumn or early spring.
The plant dies down completely in winter.

LOVAGE AND BLUE CHEESE OMELETTE

4 eggs
2 teaspoons of freshly chopped lovage
75g (3oz) blue Cheshire cheese
16g (½oz) butter

Whisk the eggs and the lovage together. Coarsely grate the
cheese. Heat the butter in an omelette pan; when foaming
pour in the egg mix. Cook over a medium heat, drawing the
back of a spoon through the omelette as it cooks to allow the

runny mix to run through to the heat. When the omelette is cooked underneath and soft and creamy on top, sprinkle with cheese; leave for a few moments until it starts to melt then fold in two and serve.

MARJORAM (*Origanum* spp)

There are three species of marjoram, each with its own distinctive flavour and uses. Sweet marjoram (*O. marjorana*) is perhaps the most useful, with a gentle spiciness. It does not bear hard cooking and its flavour is best used later in the cooking process. Use it in stuffing, where it is protected from fierce heat, or as a complement to egg or cheese dishes. Sweet marjoram is a half-hardy perennial best treated as an annual in the chilly UK climate. It carries small green leaves and white flowers, growing to just 20cm (8in) in height.

Pot marjoram (*O. onites*) has a more intense flavour, which can, if used with too heavy a hand, overpower many dishes. It fares best in robust dishes, teamed with tomatoes or spicy sausages. Pot marjoram is a hardy perennial that can reach 45cm (18in) in height. It forms a green mat in winter and in summer is smothered with tiny pink flowers.

Wild marjoram (*O. vulgare*), or oregano as it is often confusingly dubbed, has the most intense spicy and bitter flavour, which can vary hugely from one location to another. It does relish heat and may not fully achieve its flavour potential in cooler climates. Fortunately the drying process seems to enhance its properties. Its powerful taste is utilised in rich dishes from the south, often heavy with tomatoes and garlic. It is a hardy perennial with hairy green leaves that remain on the plant throughout the year; in summer it carries purple flowers (see colour section for illustration). Like pot marjoram it can reach 45cm (18in) in height. The leaves can be used fresh and retain a powerful punch when dried.

PROPERTIES: Marjoram has sedative properties and must be used with respect. It is said to soothe the digestive system, work as a diuretic and a tonic, and have antiviral properties.

CULTIVATION: Marjoram enjoys rich, well-drained soil and a sunny situation. Sweet marjoram is best sown in early spring in a seed tray under glass. The seed is very fine; you may find it easier to sow if you first mix it in with a little sharp sand. Plant out in early summer when all danger of frost has passed. Pot marjoram can be propagated by softwood cuttings taken in spring or by division in spring or autumn. Wild marjoram can be readily grown from seed or propagated by root division, again in either spring or autumn.

MINT (*Mentha* spp)

Mint, possibly the best-known herb, offers an enormous array of flavours from its many hundreds of different varieties and species. Spearmint (*Mentha spicata*), which is also known as garden or common mint, has a delightfully crisp and slightly sweet flavour and is the most frequently used culinary species. Moroccan mint is the true gourmet variety of *M. spicata* and is said to have the best flavour, which makes the best mint tea of all. Mint combines well with tomatoes and offers a sharp aside to the rich flavour of lamb, a classic British Sunday lunch combination. It can be used to make stuffings, sauces and jellies; it is the main ingredient of cocktails such as the mojito and mint julep; and it is an important ingredient in Middle Eastern cuisine. Yoghurt, garlic and mint combine to make the Greek appetiser *Tzatziki*. Mint is delicious added to vegetables, either in the cooking process or by sprinkling the chopped leaves on the serving dish – potatoes are the classic but try it with carrots, courgettes and peas, or whatever takes your fancy.

Spearmint has bright green deeply veined leaves and white flowers in summer (see colour section for illustration). Bowles mint (*M. x villosa*) has hairy leaves which are not good in salads, but tasty when cooked, as are the green-and-white variegated leaves of apple mint (*M. suaveolens*) – whose flavour is reflected in its name.

PROPERTIES: Mint has antibacterial, anti-inflammatory and antispasmodic properties. It is a common and readily available digestive aid and can help to soothe headaches. Mint oils should not be used on or around babies and pennyroyal (*Mentha pulegium*) should not be taken during pregnancy.

CULTIVATION: Mint virtually cultivates itself – checking its spread is usually more of an issue than getting it to grow. It will tolerate full sun, but really appreciates a little shade and a rich, damp soil. If it is happy you may have a fresh supply at your disposal for eight or nine months of the year. The easiest method of propagation is by root division in late winter or early spring. Pop your young plant into a pot and watch it grow. Even if you're growing mint in the border, it's still advisable to grow it in a container sunk into the ground to stop it spreading. There are many different varieties to choose from and all mint varieties freely hybridise. Whenever I have moved house and needed to establish a new supply I ask a friend or relative with a particularly luscious plant to dig up a bit of root, or simply take a chunk of root with me – that way I know for sure the quality of plant I'll be getting. Spearmint or peppermint planted near roses will deter aphids.

Mustard (*Brassica* spp)

Mustard has been a kitchen essential for many thousands of years. Mustard leaves are pungent and peppery in salads and the flowers are also edible and can be tossed into salads or popped into sandwiches. Use the young leaves (eight to ten days after sowing) for salads. There are three species: black mustard (*B. nigra*) has the strongest-flavoured seeds; white mustard (*B. alba*) is the mustard part of the mustard and cress salad crop; brown mustard (*B. juncea*) is grown for its seed, but the flavour of the seed is not released until it is ground and mixed with a liquid. To make mustard, grind dried seed and add a little water until you have a thick paste. Leave to stand for ten minutes to allow the flavour to develop – the mixture will not keep, so make fresh as required.

PROPERTIES: Mustard was used in poultices to soothe the pain and inflammation caused by arthritis and rheumatism. A mustard foot bath is said to relieve the problem of smelly feet.

CULTIVATION: Mustard enjoys a sunny situation with well-drained soil. Sow at three-week intervals for a constant supply of leaves, or sow in spring for a seed crop. To harvest seed, pick the pods before they open in late summer.

Nasturtium (*Tropaeolum majus*)

All parts of the nasturtium, that well-loved garden annual, are edible. The young leaves, which are packed with minerals and vitamin C, are hot and peppery and can be added to salads (see colour section for illustration). Nasturtium is a great companion plant because it attracts blackfly, though this is naturally a downside when it comes to consuming the flowers.

The flowers are delicious and can be added to both salads and stir fries, but please take care to clean them very thoroughly to remove any flies. The young green seeds are peppery and can be pickled and used much as capers in rich sauces. Make a pickling liquid with white wine vinegar; add salt, pepper, garlic, a little celery seed, a small chopped onion and a squeeze of lemon juice. Bring to the boil, cool, put in a bottle and add the nasturtium seeds as they form.

PROPERTIES: Nasturtium is believed to be a tonic for the digestive system for it has cleansing and antibiotic properties.

CULTIVATION: Nasturtiums enjoy well-drained soil and a sunny situation. These annuals are incredibly easy to grow; plant the seeds directly into the ground where they are to flower. They will self-seed freely in the right conditions.

ORACH (*Atriplex hortensis*)

Orach is a handsome giant of a plant that will reach 2m (6ft) in a single season and is worth growing for its looks alone. It tastes delicious, yet remains little known in the UK. The green or red leaves of this annual are heart or arrow shaped and the green or red flowers appear from summer through to autumn – the red variety is much prettier. Only young leaves should be used in spring and summer for they become bitter when old. Add them to salads or make a tasty soup. The leaves can be substituted in any recipe for spinach.

PROPERTIES: Like spinach, orach contains vitamin C and iron and is said to aid digestion.

CULTIVATION: Orach is easy to grow but needs rich garden soil. Red orach needs partial shade as its leaves easily scorch in the sun. Sow seed in drills when all danger of frost has passed; thin plants to 30cm (1ft) intervals. Seed can be tricky to germinate, which may go some way to explain why orach is not cultivated commercially. Pick off flower heads as they form, to extend the plant's life – it will quickly run to seed once it has flowered. Successive sowings ensure a constant supply.

PARSLEY (*Petroselinum crispum*)

Parsley could probably claim the title of most-used herb. It seems to have worked its way into culinary dishes all around the world, notably in Middle Eastern recipes. It blends and accentuates flavours without overpowering and is an essential ingredient in both *bouquet garni* and *fines herbes*. There is an ongoing debate over whether the flat-leaved (*P. crispum* var. *neapolitanum*) or curly-leaved (*P. crispum*) varieties are superior – gastro snobs will almost inevitably curl a lip at the curly-leaved option, which was used and abused by British housewives for decades in a coagulation of lumpy white sauces. Cookery writer Sophie Grigson has admitted that she might not be able to differentiate between the two varieties in a blind tasting if leaves were finely chopped. Cut stalks of parsley for use as required – but only snip off the odd stalk until the clump is established. Parsley tastes best in its first year of growth; clumps of bright green leaves appear on slender stalks, reaching 30–50cm (12–20in) in height. The following year it will throw up a tall flowering stem that can reach as high as 1m (3ft). If conditions are right it will self-seed.

PROPERTIES: Parsley is rich in vitamins and minerals, containing a generous helping of vitamin C as well as iron, iodine and magnesium. It is discreetly known as a 'woman's herb' for it is said to ease problems associated with menstruation and the menopause. I have quite a taste for hot parsley tea – a few sprigs in boiling water – but pregnant women should not drink it. Parsley is also known as a breath freshener: chew a sprig or two after eating garlic.

CULTIVATION: Parsley is a biennial but is best grown as an annual. Sow in late spring or early summer in well-drained soil in sunshine or partial shade. It is easy to grow, but the seeds are terribly slow to germinate. It doesn't like having its roots disturbed so use plugs or pots rather than seed trays. You might like to try soaking the seeds in warm water overnight before sowing. The later you sow the faster the seeds will germinate. Six or seven plants will produce a wonderful crop of leaves. Sow more seeds later in the summer to ensure a constant supply and put some in pots to over winter on the window sill.

POPPY (*Papaver rhoeas, P. somniferum*)

The ripe seeds, which have a sweet, nutty taste, are the only part of the plant that is edible. They can be crushed to flavour and thicken curries, added to pastry (see opposite), or sprinkled whole over the top of home-made bread before baking. Only the seeds of *P. rhoeas* and *P. somniferum* are alkaloid free, making them safe for all culinary purposes. The seed pods should be dry before the seeds are collected; if collected too early they will rapidly deteriorate. If truth be told I love my poppy plants and collect their seed for propagation – I buy bags of seed to cook with.

PROPERTIES: All parts of the plant are toxic save for the seeds of the named species above. Opium is obtained from the unripe seed case of the opium poppy (*P. somniferum*) and is used to produce the essential pain-killing drugs morphine and codeine, as well as the addictive morphine-derivative heroin.

CULTIVATION: Poppies enjoy an open, sunny situation with well-drained soil; they will self-seed freely and can become a bit of a nuisance in the flower bed. Sow seed in spring or autumn where plants are to flower and thin seedlings to 30cm (12in) intervals. Red, white or purple flowers are succeeded by the beautiful seed heads, a masterpiece of design. Foliage and stems are a grey green.

POPPY-SEED AND TOMATO TART

This recipe comes from my friend Jill Blake who produced it for a lunch party and it has since become a family favourite. These amounts are for a 23cm (9in) tart tin with a loose base.

For the pastry:
40g (1½oz) of poppy seeds
110g (4oz) of plain flour
Approximately ½ teaspoon of salt
60g (2½oz) of chilled butter, in small cubes
½ teaspoon of dark muscovado sugar
1–1½ tablespoons of cold milk

For the filling:
40g (1½oz) of butter (or olive oil)
1 large onion, chopped
2 x 400g (14oz) cans of plum tomatoes
1 teaspoon of tomato purée
Dash of red wine vinegar
½ teaspoon of caster sugar
Around 6 basil leaves, shredded, plus 6 for decoration
Salt and pepper
110g (4oz) of Wensleydale or Feta cheese

Grease then tin and line the base with baking parchment. To make the pastry, put poppy seeds in a small non-stick frying pan and shake gently on high heat until they begin to smell nutty. (Watch carefully, it only takes a minute or so and they burn easily.) Leave to cool. Sift the flour and salt into a food processor; add the butter and process in bursts until the mix resembles breadcrumbs and no lumps of butter are left. Add the sugar and poppy seeds with a quick burst (you want the seeds to retain their texture). Add the milk a spoonful at a time, again processing in quick bursts, until the mix gathers together in a crumbly pastry. This can, of course, be done in time-honoured fashion using hands and a palette knife.Roll out the pastry on a floured board: it will be very short and may need patching with water. Prick with a fork and line with parchment weighted with baking beans. Rest in the fridge for half an hour. To avoid the pastry shrinking, don't trim it to the edge of the tart tin: drape it over the sides with an overhang of about 2.5cm (1in). Trim it back to the edge of the tin with a sharp knife either just before it goes into the oven or when it's hot and fresh from the oven. Bake the pastry blind at 190°C, 375°F, gas mark 5 for 15 minutes. Remove the parchment liner and baking beans and return to the oven to dry out for about 5 minutes. Leave the case in the tart tin.

To make the filling, gently heat butter or olive oil and, on a very low heat, soften the onion until translucent – this takes about 15–20 minutes. Add tomatoes, tomato purée, red wine vinegar, sugar and shredded basil leaves and season with salt and pepper. Simmer with the lid off until reduced to a thick and gloopy mix. Purée in the processor when cooled. (The sauce can be made in advance and keeps well in the freezer or fridge if there's any left over.) Crumble the cheese into the tart case, cover with sauce and bake for 20–25 minutes.

Carefully remove from the tin when cool enough to handle.
Decorate the top with fresh basil leaves. Enjoy warm or cold.

ROCKET (*Eruca vesicaria* subsp. *sativa*)

Rocket, next to mint, is the easiest herb to grow; it germinates
readily and self-seeds freely. It has always been a prized
flavouring: Romans used both the leaf and the seed and
it was a popular kitchen herb in Elizabethan days, eaten raw
in salad much as it is today. After the Great Fire of London in
1666 rocket is said to have sprung up all over the ruins. The
leaves have a sharp, peppery taste; their flavour becomes more
robust with age. The smallest leaves are the mildest and can
be eaten solo. As the plant matures the leaves are often mixed
with other blander leaves to offset their flavoursome punch.
Rocket is also tasty in soup and pasta dishes. If left to itself,
the plant can reach 1m (3ft) in height and has deeply divided
elongated leaves and creamy yellow flowers that appear from
July to autumn (see below and colour section for illustration).

PROPERTIES: Rocket is rich in vitamins
and minerals, notably vitamin C and
potassium and was known to be helpful
in the prevention of scurvy.

CULTIVATION: Rocket appreciates a rich
soil and light shade. Sow the seed directly
into the ground in spring when all danger
of frost has passed. The leaves will be ready
to eat within six to eight weeks of sowing.
Water the plant regularly – the leaves become
bitter if not sufficiently hydrated. Rocket will
grow happily in a good-sized container.

This is my children's all-time favourite dish and it has the advantage of being incredibly quick and easy to make.

Spaghetti (enough for 2–3 people)
3 eggs
Black pepper
Cream (optional)
Olive oil
Cubes of pancetta or bacon cut into small pieces
Garlic
A handful of rocket
Parmesan or Cheddar cheese

Bring a pan of water to the boil and when it is simmering add the pasta – try to cook just the right amount. Beat the eggs in a bowl with the black pepper – and some cream, if you are not watching your weight or want a treat. Leave on one side. Then add a splash of olive oil to a frying pan and gently cook the cubed pancetta; at the last moment add the garlic and fry gently for just a minute, then remove from the heat. When the pasta is *al dente*, drain it and return to the pan, off the heat. Add the egg mix to the pasta and then the oil, pancetta and garlic from the frying pan. Mix the ingredients together: the residual heat from the pan and the pasta will cook the egg and the sauce will become creamy. If it has cooled too much you can put it on the heat for a moment – but just for a moment, you don't want to scramble the eggs! Then add a generous handful of rocket. Serve in large bowls, sprinkled with a generous helping of cheese – I like Parmesan but my children prefer Cheddar.

ROSE (*Rosa* spp)

The dog rose (*Rosa canina*) was a food source many
thousands of years ago – seeds have been found among
the remains of Neolithic women uncovered in Britain.
Rosewater, a by-product in the production of rose oil, features
in south-Asian, west-Asian and Middle-Eastern cuisine; it is
often used as a flavouring for sweet drinks and ice creams. It
is a key ingredient in authentic Turkish delight. Rosewater is
best bought readymade, but rose-hip syrup can easily be made
from hips collected from the wild and used to flavour desserts
and ice creams. For culinary purposes use old-fashioned roses
only and remove the pale base from each rose petal as this is
rather bitter. Petals can be scattered over salads, but do check
first for stray insects.

PROPERTIES: Rose hips are an excellent source of vitamins C,
B and E. In the 1930s rose hips were discovered to contain
more vitamin C than any other fruit or vegetable – 20 times
more than the equivalent weight of oranges. When fruit and
vegetable shortages began in World War II, volunteers –
principally small boys – collected rose-hips by the sackful to
be processed into rose-hip syrup that was distributed to keep
the nation healthy.

CULTIVATION: Roses like rich, well-drained soil in sun or
partial shade. Beautiful old roses are available from specialist
nurseries and the dog rose can easily be propagated from rose
hips and popped in with some hedging. Let the hips mature
in the open air before sowing them in a pot. Deadhead flowers
in the summer to promote flowering and prune the bushes in
spring, removing crossing branches and ensuring the centre of
the bush is open and airy.

900g (2lb) of cooking apples
Juice of ½ lemon
50g (2oz) of rose petals, preferably red
Sugar

Wash and roughly chop the apples and place in a pan along
with 570ml (1 pint) of water and the lemon juice. Bring to
the boil and simmer gently until soft and pulpy; strain with
a sieve lined with muslin. Rinse the rose petals, remove the
bases and dry on kitchen paper. Put 2 teaspoons of sugar into
a bowl, add the rose petals and pound until broken up. Place
in a saucepan with 150ml (¼ pint) of water and simmer for
15 minutes. Strain through muslin and add to the strained
apple-juice mixture. Measure the total amount and add 450g
of sugar to every 570ml of liquid (1lb of sugar to every pint).
Bring to the boil and simmer gently until the sugar is
dissolved then boil rapidly until setting point is reached (this
can be tested by placing a drop of jelly on a chilled plate; if it
wrinkles to the touch, setting point has been reached).

ROSEMARY (*Rosmarinus officinalis*)

Rosemary is an indispensable culinary herb. The perfume
varies from plant to plant, but all have a whiff of camphor allied
to a deep aromatic scent. It is one of the herbs in the *herbes de
Provence* mix – the others being marjoram, thyme, basil, bay,
savory, fennel, sage and occasionally a sprig of lavender.
Rosemary is perfect with rich meat such as pork and lamb,
and a sprig thrown in with some pan-fried steak enhances the
flavour. A barbecue can be transformed by using rosemary twigs

as skewers on which to cook your meat. Steeping a sprig in a bottle of wine vinegar produces flavoured vinegar. Try adding a couple of tablespoons of freshly chopped rosemary to your bread dough for superb herb bread. Rosemary is an evergreen shrub with small pointed leaves, green on top and silver beneath; it produces whorls of blue, white or purple flowers throughout summer and can reach 2m (just over 6ft) in height (see colour section for illustration). As leaves are available all year round there is no need to dry this herb.

PROPERTIES: The essential oil from rosemary has antibacterial and antifungicidal properties. It is said to be a digestive and can soothe tummy ache and sweeten the breath. Rosemary tea is delicious: pour boiling water over a sprig of rosemary – you only need a little – and add a teaspoon of honey. As a fringe benefit is it supposed to ease flatulence.

CULTIVATION: Rosemary likes a sunny, sheltered spot, ideally on a south or south-west facing wall. It can be grown from seed, but it is much easier to take softwood cuttings. Take them in late summer and plant out the following spring. It can also be layered. Prune plants after flowering in spring; rosemary stands hard pruning and can be clipped into formal hedging. It can suffer frost damage so never prune it in winter. If you live in a cold area you might prefer to keep rosemary in a pot and give it protection over winter.

SAGE (*Salvia officinalis*)

Sage is a robust herb with a warm, musky, bitter, resinous flavour with more than a hint of camphor (see colour section for illustration). It has been used for centuries, as much for its medicinal properties as its flavouring. Sage is said to aid digestion and is therefore teamed with fatty meat such as pork, goose and duck. It contains powerful antioxidants which slow spoilage, allowing it to function as a culinary preservative. Sage is used extensively in stuffing – try blanching the leaves first as this removes the bitter notes. It is evergreen so leaves are available all year round.

PROPERTIES: Sage is a natural antiseptic and was traditionally used with vinegar in compresses and poultices to ease bruising and sprains; the vinegar brings the bruise to the surface and reduces swelling, while the sage soothes and heals. It is said to soothe sore throats and has been used to help regulate periods and diminish hot flushes.

CULTIVATION: Sage likes a warm, sunny spot, in well-drained soil. A gap between paving slabs is ideal: the herb will bask in the heat thrown up by the stone. It can be grown from seed, but no leaves can be picked until it is in its second year. Faster results come from softwood cuttings taken in late spring or early summer, and layering can be used when the plant is old, straggly and woody. Cut back stems in early spring to promote bushy growth. Plants need to be replaced every five years or so.

SALAD BURNET (*Sanguisorba minor*)

This is a curious little plant with the dearest minuscule green flowers with cerise styles arranged in a globular flowering head (see colour section for illustration). The leaves have a rather nutty flavour mixed with a hint of cucumber. They are most commonly added to salads; the youngest leaves are the best to use, older leaves can become bitter and unpleasant. They can also be added to soups and stews or used to flavour summer drinks such as Pimms.

PROPERTIES: Salad burnet has astringent and diuretic properties. It is said to increase perspiration and aid digestion.

CULTIVATION: This hardy perennial can only be grown from seed, but it will self-seed freely if content in a sunny position.

SAVORY (*Satureja* spp)

Savory is believed to be one of the earliest culinary herbs; it has a strong, spicy, warm and peppery flavour that draws out the flavour of other ingredients. Summer savory (*S. hortensis*) is milder and so is generally recommended for culinary use over its stronger-flavoured relative winter savory (*S. montana*), but this is very much a question of taste. Savory features in many recipes for beans, notably broad beans: try adding a few sprigs for a hint of spiciness. Try it with other vegetables as well and use it to season fish, or slip it in with fatty meat stews that are hard to digest. It is an important flavouring in salami. Summer savory is a diminutive, aromatic hardy annual with narrow, pointed, dark green leaves and small white, pink or purple flowers that draw the bees (see colour section for illustration). Winter savory is very similar in appearance but it is a hardy perennial.

PROPERTIES: Savory is a digestive and is said to soothe stomach ache and ease wind. The crushed leaves of winter savory may help to ease the pain of wasp and bee stings.

CULTIVATION: Savory enjoys a sunny spot with light, rich soil. Sow summer savory seed directly into the ground and thin seedlings to 20cm (8in). It is an annual but will self-seed freely in the right conditions. Winter savory, a semi-evergreen perennial, is propagated from softwood cuttings.

SCENTED-LEAVED GERANIUM (*Pelargonium* spp)

Everyone is familiar with the scented geranium but few people are aware of the range of flavours, from rose to lemon, mint and nutmeg that can be obtained from the leaves of these plants. The principal culinary plant is *Pelargonium graveolens,* which has a rose-mint scent and flavour (see colour section for illustration), while *P.* 'Lemon Fancy' and *P.* 'Attar of Roses' are self-explanatory. Take great care when using these plants that you choose a suitable variety – any old scented geranium leaf will not do; *P. crispum*, for instance, will cause stomach ache.

The Victorians used to line cake tins with the leaves when baking plain sponges, impregnating them with a delicate aroma. Once you have done this you will never want to bake a sponge in summer without this simple addition. Grease and line the tins as usual, then place around 20 leaves in the bottom of the tin before pouring over the sponge mixture. When the cake is cooked, allow it to cool before removing the paper and leaves. Their subtle flavour and perfume can also be used to make fabulous sorbets, ice creams and summer drinks. One method is to scent the sugar you will be using in the recipe by popping a few leaves into a jar of caster sugar for a week or so beforehand.

PROPERTIES: Geranium oil is often used in herbal remedies to combat head lice, but always in conjunction with combing.

CULTIVATION: Scented-leaved geraniums require a sunny spot in well-drained soil. They can be raised from seed but are very easy to grow from cuttings taken in spring or late summer; pot them up and water lightly over winter. Geraniums are damaged by frost so it is a good idea to keep them in containers and move them under cover when temperatures drop.

SORREL (*Rumex* spp)

There are two species of sorrel that can be used as a culinary herb. The shield-shaped leaves of French or buckler leaf sorrel (*R. scutatus*) have a sharp flavour with a bite of lemon zest; while the lance-shaped leaves of common or garden sorrel (*R. acetosa*) are much stronger flavoured, and should only be cooked in stainless steel as they react badly to iron. The herb is popular in France, where the leaf is eaten raw in salads, gently cooked in soups and sauces and scattered over mild dishes such as omelette to give a sharp edge. It is divine with fish. Sorrel is the only green leaf that my daughter has contentedly plucked straight from the plant to consume with relish.

PROPERTIES: Sorrel is high in vitamins A, B and C and rich in potassium. It is also high in oxalic acid and should not be used by anyone suffering from bladder stones, gout, rheumatism and pulmonary complaints.

CULTIVATION: This herb appreciates a rich, acid and moisture-retentive soil in sun or partial shade. Seeds should be sown in late spring and seedlings thinned to 10cm (4in) intervals. The plant runs to seed very quickly, so make successive sowings and remove flower heads as soon as they appear. The youngest leaves have the sweetest flavour and you can keep on picking with apparently little or no impact.

WARM POTATO AND SORREL SALAD

This recipe is adapted from Hugh Fearnley-Whittingstall's book *The River Cottage Year*; it is a firm family favourite and is incredibly easy to make. Hugh recommends using Jersey Royals when they're in season and waxy potatoes later on.

Scrub about 500g (1lb) of new potatoes and boil them
in salted water until tender: don't overcook them as soggy
potatoes will spoil the salad. Wash 1–2 handfuls of sorrel,
pat dry, then strip the central veins and shred the leaves into
ribbons about 1cm (⅜in) wide. When the potatoes are cooked,
put them in a serving bowl with a generous knob of butter, a
dribble of olive oil and the shredded sorrel. Toss, gently but
thoroughly, leave to stand for a minute and then season with
salt and freshly ground black pepper. Toss again and serve.

SWEET CICELY (*Myrrhis odorata*)

Sweet cicely has the advantage of being both a delicious
herb and a beautiful plant. It resembles cow parsley with its
clusters of creamy white flowers and bright green fern-like
foliage. It has fallen out of culinary favour, which is a shame
since it has many uses in the kitchen. All parts of the plant –
the leaves, the seeds and the root – have a faint aniseed
flavour. The leaves are natural sweeteners and can be used
when cooking fruit to reduce the amount of sugar required
and dull any acidity. They can also be chopped and added to
salads or omelettes. The fresh root has a very strong flavour
and can be used in salads or cooked as a vegetable, and the
seeds can be used in desserts. Even the flowers can be
sprinkled over salads or puddings. Pick leaves fresh as
required; gather seeds when green and leave them to ripen
fully and turn brown – ripe seeds have a stronger aniseed
flavour than unripe. The roots can be dug up in autumn.

PROPERTIES: Sweet cicely has been used as a mild tonic.
The whole plant is a digestive and the seeds can be chewed
to relieve flatulence.

CULTIVATION: This hardy perennial likes light shade and rich, well-drained soil. Sow the seed in autumn and leave in a cold frame to overwinter – it needs several months of cold temperatures to germinate. When germination occurs, move the seedlings to a cool greenhouse. When plants are large enough to handle and all danger of frost has passed, pop into the ground and space at 60cm (2ft) intervals. Root cuttings can be taken in spring and autumn, and the plant can also be propagated by division in autumn when the top growth has died back. The plant will self-seed freely given the right growing conditions.

TARRAGON (*Artemisia dracunculus*)

Tarragon is an important culinary herb, one of the *fines herbes*, along with parsley, chervil and chives, and a vital ingredient in French cuisine, although it is not of French origin, but a native of Asia and southern Europe. The plant has narrow aromatic green leaves with an aniseed scent and tiny yellow flowers that bloom from late to mid-summer. Ensure that you purchase French tarragon and not Russian (*A. dracunculus dracunculoides*), which has a coarser texture and disappointing flavour. The intensity of flavour in the leaves varies through the growing season and from plant to plant and it can be overpowering, so taste regularly when using. It is best fresh, but can be frozen successfully. Add the chopped leaves or young stalks to poultry and fish, or try adding a little to mildly flavoured vegetables such as Jerusalem artichokes and marrows – their digestive properties should help soothe the wind that the Jerusalem artichokes will inevitably produce. Tarragon is an essential ingredient in béarnaise and hollandaise sauces as well as *sauce tartare*. To make tarragon

vinegar – ideal for French dressing – simply steep
tarragon stalks in warmed white wine vinegar and
leave for three weeks.

PROPERTIES: Tarragon is said to be helpful in treating all sorts
of digestive upsets, from nausea to flatulence; it is believed to
activate the flow of digestive juices. It is rich in vitamins A
and C as well as iodine and mineral salts. Like other
wormwoods, such as the silvery garden plant *A. absinthium*
(the bitter, aromatic base for the addictive liqueur absinthe), it
is still commonly drunk as a *digestif* on the continent. To make
your own version use around 900ml (1½ pints) of 40–50 per
cent proof alcohol such as vodka. Pour it into a jar, add 25g
(1oz) of fresh tarragon leaves, a vanilla pod and 350g (12oz)
golden granulated sugar. Seal the jar and leave to infuse for
a month, shaking occasionally. Remove the vanilla pod and
leaves before use.

CULTIVATION: Tarragon is a half-hardy perennial that will
reach around 1m (3ft) in height. It likes a sunny situation in
well-drained soil. It is not fully hardy and needs protection in
severe winters: cut it down and cover with a mulch of straw
or agricultural fleece. Tarragon will be content to dwell in a
good-sized container in the garden and can then be easily
tucked away for the winter. The plant does not self-seed
reliably in our temperate climate; it is best propagated by
root division or cuttings.

THYME (*Thymus* spp)

Thyme (*T. vulgaris*) has a warm, pungent aroma and a
powerful taste; it is an essential ingredient in *bouquet garni*
and can be used to flavour soups, stews and casseroles. Unlike

many herbs, it does not lose its power with long, slow cooking and it can blend with other flavours or dominate as required. Its preservative qualities have ensured its place in the cooking of salami, sausages and pâtés, and flavoured herb oils and vinegars. In hot climates the sun draws out the aromatic oils in the leaves and produces the best flavours, in cooler climates leaves may require pounding with a pestle and mortar to draw out their taste. Lemon thyme (*T.* x *citriodorus*) has the thyme flavour, but with lemony overtones that are particularly delicious with chicken. Orange-scented thyme (*T* x *citriodorus* 'Fragrantissimus') can be used in desserts as well as main dishes. Thyme is a low-growing evergreen herb. It has small, paired, oval grey-green leaves and flowers that range in colour from purple to white, depending on variety (see colour section for illustration).

PROPERTIES: Thyme contains thymol, a natural antiseptic and preservative, which makes it an effective treatment for sore throats and sore gums – it is still used commercially in the manufacture of toothpaste and mouthwash. It is also said to be helpful in easing respiratory complaints. Strong thyme tea should not be drunk during pregnancy.

CULTIVATION: Thyme likes to be dry, so it requires a sunny, sheltered, well-drained spot and will suffer in cold and wet winters – the plants often thrive planted in the cracks between paving stones. Trim plants after flowering to encourage new growth and to stop them becoming woody. Thyme is best propagated from softwood cuttings taken in spring or autumn. However, you can also try layering or sowing seed. Thyme dries well, which can be useful in winter: pick stems before the plant comes into flower and hang upside down in a dry and airy place.

THYME AND CHEESE BISCUITS

Kate Shirazi, best friend and cookie and cupcake maker *par excellence*, has given me this recipe from her book *Cookie Magic* with the warning that the biscuits are far too delicious, so watch out for your waistline.

50g (2oz) of softened butter
115g (4oz) of strong Cheddar cheese
1 teaspoon of English mustard powder
Pinch of salt
100g (3½oz) of plain flour
2 teaspoons of chopped fresh thyme

Blend the butter and cheese. Add everything else and mix to form a dough. Roll the dough into a thin log around 2–3cm (1in) in diameter. Wrap in cling film and chill for at least 30 minutes. Preheat the oven to 180°C, 350°F, gas mark 4. Line two baking trays with silicone liners. Unwrap the dough and slice into 5mm (³⁄₁₆in) thick rounds. Place on the tray and bake for ten minutes. Transfer to a wire rack to cool.

WILD STRAWBERRY (*Fragaria vesca*)

Don't confuse the wild strawberry with its bloated relative the garden strawberry (*Fragaria x ananassa*): its taste and fragrance are far more intense and concentrated. The fruit is tart, but simply sublime: a true gourmet delight. The problem is getting sufficient quantities. One solution is to freeze the fruit in tiny batches, saving it up to make jam or a perfect dessert. It freezes much better than the commercial strawberry. Although not technically a herb, all parts of the plant, including the leaves, are prized for their culinary, medicinal and other herbal qualities. The leaves are perfumed as indicated by the plant's botanical name, *fragrans* meaning fragrant, and smell of musk when dried. In appearance the fruit is similar to that of the cultivated strawberry, but altogether smaller and more delicate. The leaves are deeply veined and serrated. Plants carry tiny white flowers in late spring and the fruit follows on from summer through to autumn (see colour section for illustration).

PROPERTIES: The plant has a high iron, potassium and mineral-salt content and is helpful to anyone suffering from anaemia. Both leaves and fruit contain vitamin C. Strawberry-leaf tea is said to be a good tonic for convalescents, but it has to be said that the taste is pretty vile; mixing in other herbs, such as sweet woodruff (*Galium odoratum*) improves the flavour. Take great care when drying the leaves: toxins are created in the process and these do not disappear until the leaf is completely dry. Wild strawberries can cause an allergic reaction in some people.

CULTIVATION: The wild strawberry grows naturally in Europe, Asia and North America, but it is a shy little plant and easy to miss in the wild. It will tolerate both sunny and shady positions, but does enjoy shelter. It is best propagated by division: each plant will send out runners (individual plants thrown out by the parent plant) in spring; these can be potted up and, once established, separated from the parent. Plant at 30cm (12in) intervals. When the plant is fruiting, feed with a potash fertiliser. Wild strawberries do well in containers, window boxes and even hanging baskets. The plants do not produce fruit indefinitely, so keep a stock of young plants developing every year as replacements.

FURTHER READING

Bardswell, Frances, *The Herb Garden* (Bracken Books, 1986)

Bellamy, David, *Blooming Bellamy* (BBC Books, 1993)

Boxer, Arabella and Back, Phillipa, *The Herb Book* (Octopus, 1980)

Buczacki, Stefan, *Best Kitchen Herbs* (Hamlyn, 1995)

Carles, Emilie, *Une Soupe aux Herbes Sauvages* (Jean-Claude Simoën, 1977)

Clark, Samantha and Clark, Samuel, *The Moro Cookbook* (Ebury Press, 2001)

Eastoe, Jane, *Wild Food* (National Trust Books, 2008)

Fearnley-Whittingstall, Hugh, *The River Cottage Year* (Hodder & Stoughton, 2003)

Garland, Sarah, *Herbs & Spices* (Frances Lincoln, 1979 and Harper Collins, 2002)

Goodrick Mass, Irma, *Herbs for the Kitchen* (Little, Brown & Company, 1975)

Grigson, Sophie, *Sophie Grigson's Herbs* (BBC Books, 1999)

Kenton, Leslie, *Healing Herbs* (Ebury Press, 2000)

MacDonald, Betty, *The Egg and I* (George Mann of Maidstone, 1992; first published 1945)

McVicar, Jekka, *Jekka's Complete Herb Book* (Kyle Cathie Ltd, 1994)

Ottolenghi, Yotam and Tamimi, Sami, *Ottolenghi: The Cookbook* (Ebury Press, 2008)

Page, Mary and T Stearn, William *Culinary Herbs* (Cassell Educational, 1974)

Shirazi, Kate, *Cookie Magic* (Pavillion, 2009)

Tabor, Roger, *Herbs* (Frances Lincoln, 2002)

van Straten, Michael, *Super Herbs* (Mitchell Beazley, 2002)

Vaughan, J. G. and Geissler, C. *The New Oxford Book of Food Plants* (Oxford University Press, 1997)

AUTHOR'S ACKNOWLEDGEMENTS

I would like to thank my children Florence, Teddy and
Genevieve for their enthusiasm, encouragement and
good-natured compliance in testing the recipes in this book.
My husband Eric provides a fabulous dictionary service when
my spelling fails me and can always be relied upon to resolve
grammatical queries. Finally, I would like to thank Polly
Powell, Tina Persaud and Kristy Richardson at National
Trust Books for their faith in me.

INDEX